Christian Nurture
in the
Twenty-First Century

A New Vision for Christian
Formation

Cynthia Coe

Cynthia Coe

Christian Nurture in the Twenty-First Century: A New Vision for Christian Formation

Copyright © 2015 Cynthia Coe

All rights reserved.

Published by:

    SYCAMORE COVE CREATIONS
    KNOXVILLE

    sycamorecove.org

For information, please contact info@sycamorecove.org

ISBN-10:0692551182

ISBN-13:978-0692551189

Christian Nurture in the Twenty-First Century

Cynthia Coe

Christian Nurture in the Twenty-First Century

## CONTENTS

| | |
|---|---|
| **A Downward Spiral** | 1 |
| **Once Upon a Time in the Church** | 8 |
| **A Theology of Christian Formation for the Twenty-First Century** | 38 |
| **A New and Renewed Vision for Christian Formation** | 59 |
| **Onward and Upward** | 88 |
| **Essays on Contemporary Christian Formation** | 93 |
| **Re-Thinking "Sunday School" As We Know It: Essays on Children's Christian Formation** | 95 |
| Why Christian Formation is Important | 97 |
| "Children's Ministries" – What if We Started From Scratch? | 99 |
| Beyond Sunday School: A Five Pointed Star of Children's Christian Formation | 102 |
| Catechesis of the Good Shepherd & Godly Play: What are the Differences, and Do They Matter? | 105 |
| Re-Thinking Crafts in Children's Programs | 116 |
| Re-Thinking the Summer | 120 |
| Is It Time to Start Paying Formation Teachers? | 122 |

| | |
|---|---|
| Advocating Children's Gifts & Talents | 126 |
| Teaching About Hunger | 129 |

**Youth Ministry in the Real World: Essays on Youth Ministry in the Twenty-First Century** — **133**

| | |
|---|---|
| Youth Ministry – Remembering Who We Are | 135 |
| Confessions of a Gym Mom…or why my children (and I) didn't go to church youth group | 140 |
| Feeding Twinkies | 144 |
| Youth Ministry @ Home | 147 |
| Stop the Madness | 150 |
| Keepin' it Real | 153 |
| The Importance of Being Empowered | 156 |
| Are We On a Mission…or Just a Trip? Know Before You Go | 159 |
| What is the Purpose of Confirmation Preparation? (And Will Tech Do the Job?) | 164 |

**Adult Spiritual Growth and Discipleship:**

**Essays on Lifelong Christian Formation**     167

What Would "Missionary Society" Formation     169
Look Like?

We're Stuck – Spiritual Growth, A Lifelong Process     172

Changing Adult Hearts and Minds     175

Christian Formation of Adults –What's it
All About?     179

Lifelong Nourishing, Lifelong Transformations     183


**The Church in the Twenty-First Century:**
**Essays on Re-Thinking How We "Do" Church**     187

Garden Variety Christian Formation     189

"Spiritual Not Religious" – And If the Church     197
Were Christian

Numbers – Do They Matter? Two Arguments,     201
Pro and Con

Mustard Seeds of Faith – Why Small Churches     205
Might Not be as "Disadvantaged" as They Think

Give Peace (And Denominational Resources)     207
A Chance

Growing Seeds of Hope     212

| | |
|---|---|
| **Acknowledgements** | **217** |
| **About the Author** | **219** |
| **Notes** | **221** |

Christian Nurture in the Twenty-First Century

## A DOWNWARD SPIRAL

### CHAPTER ONE

The continuation of the Christian faith depends on the continuation of faith among human beings. The passing of the faith to future generations is at the crux of any attempts to carry on and carry out the message, witness, and ministry of Jesus Christ. The light of Christ must be passed, flame to flame, candle to candle, to new Christians in the twenty-first century if it is to be kept alight.

Though the message of Christianity is sorely needed in a world troubled by hunger, fear, war, and injustice, the social landscape of the twenty-first century works against the nurture of children in a faith that will enable them to cope with harsh realities and postmodern challenges. As church attendance dropped dramatically during the latter years of the twentieth century, it became socially acceptable for a person of high repute to utter the words, "I don't attend church." The ever increasing affluence of American culture has provided most people with a wide array of activities by which to spend their time, leaving ever-dwindling time for participation in the church or even scant attention to spiritual matters. Materialism has become rampant, and demands of the workplace have become paramount for both men and women. Violence and fear of violence have become mainstays of the culture.

Nurture of children in the life and teachings of the Christian faith becomes difficult at best in this environment. Children learn what adults have set before them as worthy of their time and efforts. Children become what they see modelled for them in adults near and dear to them. Children can only absorb and practice the faith if they are exposed to it and if it is held up as a Kingdom of God worth having. Though the message of the Good News of Jesus Christ is sorely needed in a world fraught by war, hunger and injustice, the structures that have supported the Christian nurture of children in the past are dwindling and in rapid decline.

In looking back at the two thousand year history of the Church, Christianity has been strongest when Christian formation of new Christians, including children, was given a high priority. In the early years of Christianity, the faith exploded with new, dedicated converts as church leaders put great emphasis on the ministry of teaching, held up the position of "teacher" as one of respect, and developed a process by which new Christians would learn and live the faith.

After the church became established, Christian formation was seen as no longer necessary. Europeans were baptized at birth, and no conversion or faith formation was deemed necessary. As a result, though much of Europe was nominally Christian during the medieval period, few Europeans - including the clergy - knew the basics of the faith.

The Church rebounded during the Reformation as Martin Luther, John Calvin, and other Protestant reformers reclaimed the practice of intentional, systematic processes of Christian formation. These processes carried over into American culture, with Sunday School and adult Bible studies part of the cultural landscape until the latter part of the twentieth century. America could, until the middle part of the twentieth century, be considered a "Christian" nation. Most Americans could be assumed to understand the basics of the Christian faith, if they were born into even a nominally Christian household.

That world no longer exists. Though many nominally Christian Americans are not at all versed in the basic tenets of the faith or basic stories of the Bible, most churches continue on the path of asking these same adults to serve in the all-important roles of teacher and Christian parent. Structures designed to nurture children in the faith and teach them about Christianity are based on factors and assumptions that simply no longer exist. In this new world of the twenty-first century, systems of passing on our Christian faith need to be re-thought and re-configured if they are to be of any effectiveness in passing the faith to new generations.

In undertaking any re-figuring of systems of Christian nurture and formation, attention should be turned to scripture and theology. In looking at scripture and the early tradition of the church, parents have, until recent years, been considered the primary Christian educators of their own children – a concept that has been lost on most parents now raising children. Children learn the faith from the lives and examples of their own parents – not solely from a one hour class on Sunday morning, no matter how well taught. The task of raising children in the Christian faith may, for the institutional church, be more a task of educating, inspiring, and modeling the faith first to the parents of small children, before these parents can then model the faith in their homes and in the world.

Yet a large role still exists for teachers. Throughout the history of the church, Christian formation has been at its best when it has consisted of a dual system of formation modeled and taught in the home *supplemented* by intentional programs led by those called to the ministry of teaching and dedicated to it. The vast growth in Christianity during the first several hundred years after the death and resurrection of Christ was due in large part to the efforts of catechists who focused on the ministry of teaching and whose livelihoods were supported by the church. During the resurgence of Christian formation during the Reformation, churches and schools again undertook the role of supplementing the Christian education children would first learn in the home.

The efforts of professional catechists can take place in a variety of places and times. The up-side of new circumstances and changing social factors is the wide door of opportunity for exciting new methods of Christian formation that work and are effective in this new century. The teaching of Christian education in parochial schools is a time-honored method that might be reclaimed from the Roman Catholic tradition by American Anglicans. Other structures of intentional formation of children might include weekday classes for pre-schoolers or home-schooled children, parent-child retreats, diocesan sponsored regional programs, or co-operatives formed by small parishes. Programs such as these - plus many that might not yet be developed or imagined - might serve the purpose of truly and enthusiastically nurturing children in the Christian faith, supporting those called to the ministry of teaching, and equipping these teachers and children with training, facilities, and other resources to effectively teach children basic Bible stories, traditions, liturgy and other subjects which they will need to become mature Christians and practice their faith out in the world.

No one person, family, or parish can undertake these changes or re-structure the face of Christian formation. The church is the Body of Christ. A body cannot become more fit by exercising simply one muscle group or clump of cells. A body must decide it needs to become more fit and stronger before any new fitness program can take place, then equipment, a fitness regimen, and trainers must be procured. Likewise, the church will need to undertake any revitalization of Christian formation as a body, with its leadership as the brains, the vision, and the directors of this revitalization of the body.

New hope and new opportunity loom in the third millennium of Christianity, as new generations of Christians might be nurtured in the enduring truths and timeless messages of Christ. Yet they will need shepherding to lead them towards spiritual food that will feed them. Jesus said, "I am the Good Shepherd." As followers of the Good Shepherd, Christians and Christian educators might need to raise up their heads from gnawing on dry, stale pastures and acknowledge that they might be called to new, greener pastures - or even pastures that have been left fallow for many years, now to be reclaimed. New and renewed forms of Christian nurture must be found in this new millennium to keep the light of Jesus Christ alive.

## ONCE UPON A TIME IN THE CHURCH

## CHAPTER TWO

In seeking to nurture children in the Christian faith, churches are by no means locked into the present *status quo* of institutional Sunday School classes held only on Sunday mornings and taught by volunteers. In the two thousand year history of the church, institutional Sunday Schools for children are new kids on the block. Institutional Sunday Schools taught by untrained volunteers are, in fact, at odds with traditions of nurturing children in the faith established in the early years of Christianity and with theologies of Christian nurture continuing up through the nineteenth century.

Challenges faced in the twenty-first century by Christian educators, parents, and clergy are not new. Martin Luther, in the sixteenth century, bemoaned the lack of time parents had to teach their own children the Christian faith, and he strived to find new ways to teach children basic doctrine and stories while still upholding the role of parents in Christian nurture.[1] Martin Luther perhaps looked back to an earlier time in the life of the Church, when adult Christians had themselves been nurtured in the faith by a systematic process which both they and the Church took seriously.

Once upon a time in the Church, nearly two thousand years ago, parents were the primary Christian educators of their own children. Parents underwent a process of Christian formation themselves, and they then knew what to teach their children and could address moral and doctrinal dilemmas as they presented themselves in real life, out in the world and in the home. Teachers in the church were respected and supported financially by their faith communities. Teaching was a high priority, and the church grew strong because of it.[2]

*Christian Formation - The Early Years*

A mandate for early Christian education of children was set by Jesus himself. "Truly I tell you, whoever does not receive the kingdom of God as a little child will never enter it."[3] Jesus further set the tone for Christian nurture of children by the simple yet profound gesture of reaching his arms out to them and beckoning them to come to him. "Let the little children come to me, and do not stop them; for it is such as these that the kingdom of heaven belongs."[4] In rebuking his disciples' efforts to keep children away, Jesus demonstrated that children are important, children are worthy of attention, children are indeed capable of encountering Jesus and are entitled to this encounter.

As faith development psychologists later verified,[5] children already possess the qualities of faith for entering the kingdom of heaven and set the standard to which adults must later strive in their own journeys of faith.[6] Development of this natural spirituality[7] was a task given high priority by Jesus. He emphatically outlined the consequences of botching the task of leading children to God, saying that if we become "stumbling blocks" to children, we would be better off tying a millstone around our neck and jumping into the sea.[8] Clearly, the task of Christian nurture of children was set by Jesus as one of utmost importance and to be taken very seriously.

The task of teaching by the apostles after Jesus' death, resurrection and ascension, however, focused almost exclusively on adults. In the very early missionary years of Christianity, apostles undertook the primary task of spreading of the Gospel to Jews and others who likely had no prior experience with Christianity. "Education" in the church necessarily focused on adults, with the education of children left as derivative of that given their parents.[9] In a world where the adults knew nothing of Christ, the formation of parents was overwhelmingly the first priority.

Yet children were not left completely out of the Christian formation process. In the very early church, whole households were baptized together.[10] At that time, the family and all other household members (children, extended family and servants) entered the Christian community and life in Christ together. It was unthinkable that the choice to become a Christian would be made individually and without the family unit or household unit.[11] Though this was due mostly to patriarchal family systems of the time, this conversion of the household as a unit also demonstrated the radical and communal nature of the Christian faith.

The process by which adults prepared for this conversion was taken very seriously and led by specialists. Those interested in becoming Christians were required to undergo a three year formation process known as the catechumenate. As part of the catechumenate, the would-be Christians – "catechumens" – would receive instruction on Christian doctrine and this distinctive way of life. Catechumens would examine their own lives as well, making changes in pagan practices that would be incompatible with Christianity and perhaps even changing their means of livelihood.[12]

The catechumenate process was led by "catechists," teachers who might be ordained or members of the laity.[13] There is strong evidence in both scripture and in early church documents that these teachers were "specialists" whose livelihoods were supported by early Christian communities. In the Letter to the Galatians, Paul urges the faith community to "share in all good things" with their teachers.[14] An annotation in the New Revised Standard Version of the Bible states that this may be interpreted as the church's obligation to support its teachers.[15] Similarly, *The Didache*, a very early church document thought to contain the teachings of the first twelve apostles and based on the sayings of Jesus, states, "every genuine teacher is, like a laborer, entitled to his support."[16] Christians are then urged to take the first fruits of the harvest, of livestock, and of money, cloth and oil, and give them to the prophets.[17]

Teachers were, in the early church, given high respect by their faith communities and recognized as having special gifts. The Apostle Paul, in his writings, notes at several points the special gifts of teachers. In 1 Corinthians 12:28 (NRSV), for instance, teachers are listed behind only apostles and prophets in Paul's list of gifted leaders in the church.[18] Notably, teachers are indeed listed as a distinct category of leader; not every member of the Body of Christ or every leader is seen as having the gift of teaching. The author of the Letter of James goes a step further by explicitly setting teaching apart as a ministry subject to very high standards. "Not many of you should become teachers, my brothers and sisters," he writes, "for you know that we who teach will be judged with greater strictness."[19]

*The Didache*, thought to have been written in the last years of the first century of Christianity, puts teachers in the highest class of church officials. The system of leadership implied by *The Didache* consists of two categories: 1) bishops and deacons, and 2) prophets and teachers.[20] The bishops and deacons held appointed positions; teachers and prophets had spiritual gifts.[21] In cautioning early Christians that bishops and deacons were not to be slighted by teachers and prophets, we might assume that teachers and prophets held even higher esteem in the early church than those appointed by the apostles as church officials.[22]

Within the category of teachers and prophets, *The Didache* tells us of three kinds of teachers: 1) apostles, who were itinerant missionaries, 2) prophets, those who spoke in ecstasy, and 3) catechists.[23] All these teachers were to be welcomed, shown hospitality, and supported with food and lodging. Yet strict standards were applied to these teachers. Those who did not live up to their own teachings were seen as false prophets, and these teachers were held to professional standards of what kinds of support they could accept.[24]

Despite this high professionalism among teachers of adults, children were not left completely out of the picture. The Christian nurture of children was still derivative of that given to their parents, but it was not forgotten by any means. As heads of households and as mothers and fathers, new Christians were to teach their children the Christian faith themselves. *The Didache* instructs them, "[d]o not withdraw your hand from your son or your daughter, but from their youth teach them the fear of God."[25] Just as Jewish parents were instructed centuries before in the *Shema* to talk with their children of the words of the scriptures "when you are at home and when you are away,"[26] early Christian parents were expected to nurture their children by actively and personally teaching their children the faith in the course of ordinary, daily life and by first loving them.

St. John Chrysostom, Bishop of Constantinople in the fourth century, assigned to parents a sacred responsibility for the religious and moral formation of their children.[27] Parents were, in his view, the natural teachers of their children and were to reveal the image of God in their children.[28] The household was to be a "little church," and parents were to set for their children a "pattern of life."[29]

The necessity of raising children in the Christian life and faith from an early age – rather than letting such enculturation lapse until adulthood – and the high standards and importance given teachers in the early church speak to the critical importance of Christian formation in a world that generally did not know Christ. The top priority of the church in the first three centuries of Christianity was, fundamentally, Christian education.[30]

The efforts made by teachers of adults in the early church, combined with the enculturation of children by new Christian parents, were overwhelmingly successful. In the fourth century, even the Roman Empire became Christian. By the year 500, there were few adults left to be baptized into the Christian faith in Western Europe.[31] From that time on in Western Civilization and up until the late twentieth century, children would be raised and immersed in the Christian faith from birth.

*The Medieval Slump*

Early Christian education became institutionalized and formalized as the infant church developed. The highly effective catechumenate process that has served the church so well became systematized in the third and fourth centuries,[32] with a three year time period as standard and a three stage curriculum of instruction: general instruction in Christian living, intensive instruction in the Gospel, and finally mystagogy, or sacramental instruction.[33] A Catechetical school was formed in Alexandria, Egypt, in the second century, providing Christian education and training in conversing with educated non-Christians.[34] Gregory of

Nyssa wrote *The Great Catechism* in the fourth century, giving practical instruction to teachers in the church.[35] Augustine of Hippo wrote his treatise, *The Teacher*, in which he discussed techniques and attitudes teachers might assume in order to facilitate learning.[36]

Then, after accomplishing perhaps the greatest conversion effort in the history of the world, the church's efforts to convert the average member of Western Civilization virtually ceased. The catechumenate process passed out of existence in the early middle ages. From about the sixth century, the church had no system or process of training adults or children. Even as Christianity took hold over Western Europe and even as a high level of scholarship took place in monasteries and in schools and universities established by the church, the majority of people in Western Europe could not even comprehend the celebration of the Eucharist.[37]

Much of this decline in "formal" catechesis might be attributed to the newly prevailing practice of infant Baptism, rather than adult Baptism, and the church's failure to readjust its catechetical efforts accordingly. As newborns were initiated into the Body of Christ, the practice of requiring a lengthy period of formal instruction lapsed.[38] Catechesis then became the responsibility of parents and godparents, and religious education took place primarily in the home, as did vocational training and other types of learning.[39]

The church did little, however, to assist parents in the religious education of their children. As late as the ninth century, the church provided no provisions whatsoever for the training of infants after their Baptism.[40] By the twelfth century, godparents accepted within the liturgy of a child's Baptism the responsibility of teaching children a few basics of the faith (such as the creed, the Lord's Prayer, and the Ave Maria) and to take on essential moral teachings of the church.[41] The *Sarum Manual*, printed in 1543, prescribed for English parents a broader curriculum of teaching children about chastity, justice, and charity – along with the duty to teach them the Lord's Prayer, the Hail Mary, and how to sign themselves with the sign of the cross. Interestingly, the *Sarum Manual* also specified that the godparents must know these things themselves first[42] – surely a sign that a lack of knowledge on the part of these adults was a possible issue before a child was baptized.

The decline in understanding in these and other basics of the Christian faith among most adults in medieval times was, quite simply, due to the church's failure to adjust to radically different circumstances than those experienced in the early years of the church.[43] The church did not make changes that were inevitably necessitated by the huge shift from the task of converting non-believers to the task of nurturing children born into Christian households. The church's failure to make this shift resulted in the beginnings of Christianity lived nominally and without a true understanding of the faith.

*Reformation in Christianity, Reformation in Christian Formation*

As a groundswell of discontent arose with the laity's (and even clergy's) woeful ignorance of the basics of the faith, reformers of Christianity in the sixteenth century took on anew the task of intentional, systematic Christian formation. Martin Luther complained that even the bishops did not know the Gospel,[44] and movements arose all over Europe and in England to make Bibles in the vernacular available to the average person and to assist the average Christian in learning the faith.[45]

Christian formation "worked" again. Both Martin Luther and John Calvin reclaimed the dual-track model of formation that had worked so well in the early church: Christian nurture in the home by parents combined with intentional, systematic and prescribed methods of formation led by specialists. Christianity became revitalized, and for the first time in centuries, the average Christian could again know, understand, and live the basics of the faith.

Luther and other German and Swiss reformers began their efforts of renewing nurture of children in the Christian faith by looking at the example of the *Kinderfragen* (children's questions) of the Bohemian Brethren, dating back to around 1502 and appearing in German translations in 1522.[46] A catechetical poster was produced in Switzerland in 1525, which was used in homes, schools, and churches to teach children the basics of the faith. After this poster appeared, a number of catechetical products were made available by printers for use in Christian education.[47]

Frustrated with the ignorance of both parents and clergy, Luther himself wrote his *Small Catechism* in 1529, publishing parts of it on posters to be disseminated to local parishes, homes, and schools. The poster was an instant success and was eagerly adopted all over Western Europe.[48] In Switzerland, under Calvin's influence, primers were first published in 1545 to introduce children to both learning in general and to practices of piety. In writing to the Lord Protector of England in 1548 on the subject of catechetical instruction, Calvin advised, "there ought to be a common formula of instruction for little children and ignorant people that serves to make them familiar with sound doctrine so that they may discern it amidst the lies and corruptions which may be introduced to the contrary."[49]

While Luther and Calvin both heavily emphasized the role of the family and parents in nurturing children in the Christian faith, they also advocated the supplementation of this nurturing by teachers. Luther wrote his *Small Catechism* with parents in mind, and in the preface of the first edition in 1529, he urged heads of households to work with children and servants at least once a week in learning the basics of the faith.[50] He firmly pointed to parents as "bishops" in their own homes and placed upon them the responsibility for their children's spiritual well-being.[51] Yet, Luther also faced realities and addressed them head-on, writing in 1524, "Even if parents had the ability and desire to do it themselves, they have neither the time nor the opportunity for it, what with their other duties and the care of the household."[52]

Luther thus strongly advocated catechetical education as an important part of public school education, where children could develop Christian character under the tutelage of professional schoolmasters using a variety of educational methods.[53] These efforts were not to supplant the role of the parents but to better equip children to teach their own offspring and model Christianity in their own homes as they matured and formed families of their own.[54]

The role of catechist within the church structure was also reclaimed by reformers during the sixteenth century. Along with advocating catechetical instruction in public schools, Luther also established the office of catechist in Wittenberg in 1521.[55] Calvin similarly instituted the office of "teaching doctor" within the ecclesiastical hierarchy in Geneva.[56] Beginning in 1541, parents in Geneva were to take their children to catechetical instruction every Sunday at midday for sessions led by ministers entrusted with this task.[57] In Germany, clergy themselves were urged to reclaim the teaching ministry of the church – and with great success. In 1530, at the Diet of Augsburg, both boys and girls were said to pray, believe, and speak of God and Christ more than in the monasteries or schools of past days.[58]

Perhaps more importantly, Christian formation was seen as a lifelong process.[59] Catechesis was not just for children. Adults, too, were expected to study the Catechisms and scriptures and to attend worship services and hear sermons. The reformers of the sixteenth century wisely recognized that for the faith to continue, the process of Christian formation would need to continue in each person at each stage of life.

## The Anglican Middle Way

### Straddling the Fences and Falling Between the Cracks

Reforms in Christian formation made on the continent touched England but not with the force or exuberance of reform efforts in Germany and Switzerland. The dual models of family as the primary Christian nurturer of children, along with very intentional and systematic efforts led by catechists or professional teachers, were evident in England and its American colonies during the reformation and beyond, yet neither of these models have yet to be fully embraced and prioritized by Anglicans. As a result, Christian formation in the Anglican Church has flirted with both models of formation, with neither model fully supported or used effectively.

The first editions of the English *Book of Common Prayer*, published in 1549 and 1552, adopted a typical late medieval prescription of Christian formation for children. When a child was baptized, parents were charged with the duty of raising their child in the Christian faith and were specifically charged with teaching children the Creed, the Lord's Prayer, the Ten Commandments, and "other things a Christian man ought to know and believe to his soul's health."[60] Children were generally to be brought up to lead a godly and Christian life. This instruction was to be done solely within the bounds of the family.

As the reformation in England progressed, reformers continued to point to the family, and particularly mothers, as the primary and sole instructors of children in the Christian faith. All parents, mothers and fathers, were to be "a bishop in their own house."[61] Families were to undertake a program of daily study and meditation, yet other than the Prayer Book Catechism, families were given little instruction or guidelines from the church hierarchy on how precisely this Christian formation might be undertaken.[62]

Due to the new popularity and use of the printing press, however, a number of commercial printers undertook to step into this gap and provide families with numerous "primers" and "manuals" to assist children in learning the Christian faith.[63] With the exception of a primer authorized by Henry VIII in 1545 and another authorized under the auspices of Edward VI in 1553, none of these primers were in any way sanctioned or approved for use by the Church of England.[64] There was in England no comprehensive or unified program for religious education.[65]

In colonial Virginia, however, some attempts were made at intentional, professional religious education similar to those undertaken by reformers on the continent. Although Anglican Virginians considered Christian formation the duty of the parents[66] the

Assembly of the Commonwealth of Virginia nonetheless in 1661 revived the office of "lay reader," whose duty was to catechize the children. The Virginia Assembly also required that every clergyman spend a half hour each Sunday catechizing "youth and ignorant persons." [67]

Similarly, in New England, efforts were made to provide each parish with two ministers: one to provide exhortation and inspiration, and another to serve as a teacher to preach informative sermons, explain the scriptures, and to catechize the children. It was also common in colonial America for clergy to serve as schoolteachers and to include catechesis as part of the regular school curriculum.[68]

Back in England, a movement began which would revolutionize Christian formation – the Sunday School. Initially developed in Gloucester by Robert Raikes as a means of providing literacy training for poor children, the Sunday School also became an important means of providing religious instruction to poor children, as well as teaching them manners and proper hygiene.[69] The Church of England hierarchy would officially have nothing to do with the Sunday Schools, however, condemning them for giving the laity and the poor too much control and for threatening to undermine the interests of the wealthy in keeping an endless supply of cheap labor.[70]

One of the few Anglican clergy who even gave the

Christian Nurture in the Twenty-First Century

Sunday School a close look was John Wesley, who went on to make the Sunday School model a primary element in the Methodist movement that eventually became the Methodist Church. Wesley put a great emphasis on the Christian nurture of children, giving it a high priority in the Methodist Society. Wesley simultaneously endowed the home and family with a central role in a child's Christian formation. The Methodist Sunday Schools were to work hand and hand with Christian nurture by the family, not replace the parents' efforts.[71]

Parents were to meet periodically with church stewards of the Sunday School to discuss their child's progress, and parents were very intentionally linked and included in the formation process. Manuals and tracts to be read to children were published and distributed to parents. This Christian education process was considered a lifelong task, with small group meetings held for adults as a primary feature of the Methodist movement.[72]

The Sunday School became very popular with other denominations as well, particularly evangelical movements. In the early years of the movement, at least one group, the Baptist Sunday School Society, provided financial support to pay teachers. By 1794, however, most Sunday School teachers were volunteers.[73]

Anglicans eventually joined the Sunday School movement, with the first Sunday School formed in

Philadelphia in 1791 by Bishop William White. However, Episcopal Sunday Schools were met with criticism almost from the start. In the nineteenth century, Episcopal Sunday Schools were said to be "inadequate," with education either in the home or in a parochial school thought to be a preferable method of Christian formation. By 1865, the Committee on Christian Education of the Episcopal Church pointed to the deplorable state of untrained teachers in the church and suggested that schools release children for one or two hours a week to be educated by their priests.[74]

The national Episcopal Church did not take any measures to improve the state of Christian education programs in parishes, however. The few efforts to improve the state of Christian formation were entirely local in nature. Bishop Henry C. Potter of New York, for instance, formed a commission in 1898 to train teachers and uphold Sunday Schools as serious endeavors. Teachers were trained in scripture, the *Book of Common Prayer*, child development, and pedagogy. A standard curriculum was proscribed, and manuals were produced as teaching tools.[75] However, many parishes in the Episcopal Church simply did not put a high priority on Christian education of children, perhaps viewing the Sunday Schools as too closely associated with the more fundamentalist and evangelical denominations.

Christian Nurture in the Twenty-First Century

During this same time period, a movement was afoot to again point to parents and the home as the primary Christian educators of children, marked by the publication of the landmark work *Christian Nurture* by Congregationalist minister Horace Bushnell.[76] In this popular and highly tauted work, Bushnell reclaimed from early Christianity the notion that Christian nurture begins at home and with a child's parents. Parents must pass on God's love to their children from birth, teaching the child Christian values and concepts through their own actions. Children should grow up with a joyous view of religion, rather than having religion presented as oppressive and stifling[77] – a reaction surely to rote methods employed by many Sunday Schools and to various strains of Calvinism that led some churches to claim that children needed to repent and be "saved."

These competing methods of children's Christian education left Anglicans in the twentieth century attempting to straddle two fences – one of institutionalized, intentional Christian formation and the other of formation done solely in the home – yet not doing a particular good job at either. The Episcopal Church in the early part of the twentieth century made some attempts at intentional efforts to teach the basics of the faith to children. The *Christian Nurture Series* was produced in 1916, emphasizing social concerns and the needs of others.[78] In the early years of the twentieth century, Christian education classes were led by deaconesses, who in effect were church professionals.[79]

During the middle years of the twentieth century, the Episcopal Church's publishing house produced both a teaching series for adults and a comprehensive curriculum for children.[80] However, these efforts came before the rapid decline in attendance experienced by mainline Protestant churches and were discontinued precisely at the beginning of widespread disillusionment that would culminate in rampant anti-institutionalism during the last years of the twentieth century.

Recent thought on how to contend with dropping attendance rates in Christian formation and difficulties in providing quality teaching to children has, generally speaking, fallen into two camps. The first camp might be described as the "faith is caught rather than taught" school of thinking. A main proponent of this school of thought is the Rev. Dr. John H. Westerhoff, III, who has written rather disparagingly of the Sunday School model of Christian education, citing the difficulty of small churches to adequately provide a quality "school" model of Christian formation.[81] Westerhoff and others have suggested that parishes instead simply let children learn the faith by participating in church activities, with few or no efforts to present to them the basics of the faith in an intentional, age appropriate manner.[82]

The polar opposite of this school of thought currently practiced today is evidenced by several programs of Christian formation for children which are very intentional and very specific as to age appropriateness. These programs - which include *Catechesis of the Good Shepherd*[83] and *Godly Play*[84] - are led by trained teachers or catechists, use a very prescribed curriculum and methodology, and offer a "standard," tried-and-true formula followed worldwide. These programs are very popular and supported enthusiastically by their devotees, despite the cost of materials and teacher training required.

Other print curricula are also available, such as the *Episcopal Children's Curriculum* and *Living the Good News*, but the quality of programs based on these curricula might vary widely depending on the existing teaching skills leaders and teachers bring to the effort. A few parishes offer a catechumenate process for adults, but no church-wide curriculum exists for such an undertaking.

At the turn of the twenty-first century, just as the teaching ministry of the church has become a critical means of reaching out to non-Christians and nominal Christians, the Episcopal Church has no mandated or even recommended curricula, no national church-supported resources to train and support teachers, and no unified vision of what Christian formation might be in this new century. The availability of quality Christian education for those who seek to deepen their faith or even learn the basics of Christianity is tied to the enthusiasm of a particular parish or rector and what each individual parish is willing to offer. Those living in areas where leadership, vision, effort, and resources are not in evidence likely will find meager offerings, no offerings, or offerings which are poorly led or totally irrelevant to their needs and concerns.

Also, in the twentieth century, the Sunday School method seems to have lulled parents into relying solely on the institutional model of Christian education for children, while their own efforts in the home have dropped to non-existent in many families. Schools and professionals are now seen as the primary – if not only – means of educating children in religion (or anything else).[85] Myriad curricula and teaching aids are available in this culture of internet commerce and affluence, but parents are no longer held in any way accountable for even driving their children to Sunday School, much less for their child's spiritual well-being.

Christian Nurture in the Twenty-First Century

*The Social Landscape of the Twenty-First Century*

As the Church moves into the twenty-first century, several cultural factors seriously affect the course of Christian nurture and formation of children – and Christianity itself. These factors have pushed current means of providing Christian formation to children (as well as adults) to the point of near-obsolescence. Several of these factors are similar to those faced by church leaders in the years prior to the Reformation. Other factors, however, would be more familiar to the apostles and catechists of the infant church of the third and fourth centuries.

A problem facing the church which is almost identical to that faced by Martin Luther and his contemporaries is the increasing inability of parents to personally and solely raise their children in the Christian faith, despite best intentions. In this new age of the social acceptability of non-attendance at church, many adults may well have grown up without a religious education themselves.[86] They may not have studied the Bible at all, and any liturgy used by a particular denomination might leave them mystified out of ignorance, rather than any spiritual effect.

A sheer lack of time as parents are preoccupied with other responsibilities or activities is also a huge factor leaving adults little time to actively and intentionally teach their children about the Christian faith. Involvement in church related activities, such as Bible study groups and church social events, has dropped to participation by only one in eight Americans – a drop from participation by one in three Americans in the 1960s and one out of two in the 1950s.[87]

If they do serve as volunteers, mainline Protestants and Roman Catholics are more likely to be involved as volunteers in the secular community than in their home parishes.[88] In an era of increasing individualism and a dizzying array of ways to spend one's time, Americans are generally losing interest in volunteer organizations of any kind, secular and religious.[89] "I don't have time" is given as the primary reason Americans give most often when asked why they don't participate in community organizations.[90]

Along with rapid declines in the amount of time the average parishioner might have to personally teach a child or devote volunteer time to Sunday School teaching is a parallel trend in American culture towards professionalization of many activities heretofore done primarily or even solely by volunteers. Most middle to large cities offer a plethora of for-proft programs for children taught by professionals, including karate lessons, gymnastics classes, science lessons, art lessons, music lessons, and numerous other camps and after-school care programs. The expectation of parents bringing their children to church school on Sunday morning is likely the same expectation they have when they dropped their children off at these for-profit programs: that "professional" teachers would be there to completely take over the task and do it with professional standards, without any help at all from "amateur" parents.

This professionalization of children's activities has crippled parents' abilities to develop skills and relationships with their own children. As children are shuffled from one activity to another, the parents are very decidedly NOT spending time with their own children. In a hectic but relatively affluent day and age, it is much easier to write out a check for child care than to spend the energy it takes to teach a child the everyday skills of patience, of generosity, of respect for others, of taking time for rest and for the development of one's spiritual life. Christian nurture of the kind espoused by St. John Chrysostom and Horace Bushnell becomes impossible.

Parents themselves have begun to express and identify their own inabilities to teach their own children basic values[91] - a first step, perhaps, in working back to a Bushnellian approach of parents modeling faith to their children. According to a study by Public Agenda, a non-profit research organization, parents do not believe they are doing a very good job teaching their children essential values, ranging from self-discipline to basic manners.[92] Similarly, parents are inundated with so-called "expert advice" to the extent that many parents do not feel competent to raise their own children.[93]

Research of Protestant denominations has detected a feeling of incompetence on the part of parents specifically with respect to religious up-bringing.[94] Breakdowns in community, resulting from a lack of time on the part of parents, have also contributed to a lack of opportunities for parents to simply speak with each other on issues of parenting. Even if they had these opportunities, there would be no guarantee whatsoever that the advice they might give or receive would have any grounding at all in Christian theology.

The long era of Christendom dating back from the triple digit years of the last millennium is over,[95] and churches cannot assume that adults will ever attend church, even after they become parents. The parents of most small children growing up in these first years of the twenty-first century are highly suspicious - if not hostile - to institutional religion, and many of them no longer attend church or never attended church in the first place.[96] These young adults, now approaching middle age, typically put little stock in religious institutions and, as alternatives, look for icons of spirituality and discussions of theology within pop culture.[97] They see prophecy in all believers (whether in or out of the church),[98] and they follow a type of liberation theology, seeking to liberate Jesus from the chains of organized religion and seeking what is "true" amongst all the hierarchy and inadequacies of the church.[99]

Anti-institutionalism is nothing new. Anti-institutionalism has been snowballing since at least the 1960s and 1970s.[100] What is new is that anti-institutionalism has become mainstream. At some point, probably in the 1980s – as Generation Xers were reaching their teen years and adulthood – anti-institutionalism directed towards the church hit a "tipping point" and rose to epidemic proportions.[101] What is new is that young adults can and will without hesitation say to the church, "no thank you" if the church does not meet their needs. What is new is that young adults will likely have nothing to do with the church unless the church meets them where they are.

In this respect, challenges currently faced by church leaders are more similar to those faced by early Christian missionaries to the unchurched. In this respect, church leaders might well look to approaches used by the early church to convert and form adults and children in the Christian faith, rather than continue on with programs and approaches designed for a culture already converted. The Great Commission Jesus gave his apostles, "Go ye into all the world and preach the Gospel" might well be understood by church leaders of the twenty-first century as the world right around them, the world where their next door neighbors might know little or nothing of the Christian faith.

*Using the Gift of Hindsight*

New means of reaching future generations of Christians might, then, be ways the church has "done" Christian formation in the past. Ironically, Christianity might be re-vitalized by methods of the very early church and by reclaiming the practices and theologies of Christian formation from periods in church history in which Christianity was vital and growing in new ideas and fresh perspectives. As Christianity moves into its third millennium, we have the marvelous gift of hindsight to look back on efforts to strengthen the faith and to see what "worked" and what did not work.

What "worked" was holding parents up as the primary Christian educators of their own children at birth and charging them with the responsibility of teaching them the basics of the faith throughout their youth.

What "worked" was strong supplemental support of families by systematic, intentional efforts provided by the church and led by trained teachers. When children were given both of these types of nurture, working hand-in-hand, the average Christian knew the scriptures, understood rites of worship, and could live the faith out in the world on a day to day basis.

Cynthia Coe

# A THEOLOGY OF CHRISTIAN EDUCATION FOR THE TWENTY FIRST CENTURY

## CHAPTER THREE

In setting a path for Christian nurture of future generations, "what works" might be found in starting with a theological approach to Christian formation of children. In assigning the task of raising children in the Christian faith, models for who should teach and model the faith to children are readily found in scripture. From scripture can be formed a theology for Christian nurture in the twenty-first century that is both innovative - meeting the needs of parents and cultural forces affecting them - and fully consistent with ancient traditions and Biblical principles.

The direction of Christian formation of children in recent years has often veered sharply from theological and scriptural bases. Instead, vision for Christian education has often amounted to what looks easy for the average overburdened volunteer or comes packaged in an attractive box. Clergy might be too busy with other ministries to set a clear direction for the Christian nurture of children or might defer to lay members with no theological education or with no formal training in

Christian education at all. Parents are often left out of the equation entirely. Parents, instead, typically drop their children off at the Sunday School door, thinking "the church" will provide all the religious education their children need.

Faith communities rarely enter into theologically based discussions to address root issues driving their Christian education programs. Is the church supposed to provide all the Christian formation a child might need, and if so, in what form? What role are the parents to play in any intentional, systematic Christian formation the church might provide? What is the role of church Christian education staff? And who decides what is taught, how it is taught, and by whom?

All of these questions should be asked and answered with reference to theology. "What worked" in the past was done so with regard to strong reference to scripture and with strong theological basis. What will work in future years will likely succeed only if the church, clergy, Christian educators, and parents themselves seek again to re-connect the direction of Christian nurture to scripture and theology.

*Parents Are the Primary Christian Educators of Their Own Children - A Concept Older Than Christianity*

In Jesus' time, the concept of who was responsible

for the religious and spiritual upbringing of children was not an issue. It was the parents. In the *Shema*, the faithful are instructed to love the Lord their God with all their hearts, with all their souls, with all their might, and to keep these words in their hearts.[102] In the next breath, they are told to recite these words to their children.[103]

The *Shema* proscribes a holistic approach to the religious education of children. Religious education does not consist of simply sitting children down at a certain time and drilling scripture verses into their heads. Parents are exhorted to talk about these words in the home and when they are away.[104] These words become the way people of faith live their lives and the way they raise they children - enculturation.

Not only are parents exhorted to teach their children by passing down certain words and concepts to them,[105] they are to stand prepared to answer their questions as well. The author of Deuteronomy anticipated children asking questions about God, about salvation, and God's work in our lives. In Deuteronomy 6:20, the author refers to a time "*when* your children ask you...," not *if* they ask you. Questions are to be answered with specific stories, particular answers - not with "honey, I don't know" or "ask your Sunday School teacher." Parents are asked to witness. Parents are expected to have something to say about God to children when they are asked.

These Old Testament concepts are part of the Christian heritage and concepts that were continued in the early church, as the authors of the *Didache* likewise appointed parents as the primary Christian educators of their own children. This concept was then re-iterated by St. John Chyrsostom in the fourth century and later by Horace Bushnell in the late nineteenth century.

For Episcopalians, this theology of parents as the primary Christian educators of their own children is at the heart of the Rite of Baptism. When a child is presented for Baptism in an Episcopal church, the priest asks, "will you be responsible for seeing that the child you present is brought up in the Christian faith and life?" The *parents* say the words, "I will, with God's help."[106]

The parents do not, according to the 1979 Book of Common Prayer, get away with simply teaching their children the Lord's Prayer, a Creed, and the Ten Commandments, as they did in the past. Instead, the parents are charged with the responsibility of helping the child "to grow into the full stature of Christ" – a hugely comprehensive task requiring a great deal of effort and conscientiousness on the part of the parents (or others who may present the child for Baptism).[107]

The congregation is also asked to support those about to be baptized by pledging to "do all in [their] power to support these persons in their life in Christ" – a pledge made in addition to that made by the parents. This charge to the faith community is likewise comprehensive and holistic. The drafters of the 1979 Baptismal Rite clearly envisioned the parents as the specific members of the congregation primarily responsible for Christian formation. At no point in the Baptismal Rite does the parish vow to do it for them. "Support" means a supplemental role, not a substitution.

This theology of parents as the primary Christian formation leaders of their own children is well rooted in the Gospel. In the Gospel according to Matthew, Jesus says, "[w]hoever welcomes one such child in my name welcomes me."[108] When parents present their child for Baptism, they are in fact welcoming that child in Christ's name. This welcome surely means introducing this child to the household of God and all that this might encompass. Welcoming the child to the Body of Christ, to this Christian household, including showing the child what this household is about, who is in this household, what is expected in the household, and what the place of the child in this household might be – the same introduction parents make when a child is brought into their earthly household.

## Christian Nurture in the Twenty-First Century

The parents are, for a child presented for Baptism, the doorkeepers and the earthly hosts of the child as it grows into the full stature of Christ. The parents must bring the child into the Christian community in the first place; a newborn infant or small child does not approach the Baptismal font alone and ask to be a member of the faith community. The child must be made to feel welcome, both in its earthly home and in the faith community, and the parents' attitudes will have a lot to do with whether the child does indeed feel welcome, secure, and joyful as a member of its family and of the faith community.

The faith community has a simultaneous role to play in welcoming the child. In this respect, the availability of Christian formation classes will not be the sole factor in supporting the child in his or her life in Christ. More important factors are whether members of the faith community smile at the child, welcome the child during worship services and at parish social events, and quite simply how the other members of the parish, young and old, relate to the individual child.

The role of formal Christian formation classes is not inconsistent with the role of parents as primary Christian educators. Formal, intentional classes provided by the faith community as only one facet of a child's Christian formation which must work in concert with what is happening in a child's home and in a child's world. Formation is not by any means a process that happens only in the classroom.

*Christian Formation Begins At Birth*

The role of parents as primary Christian educators might include a broad number of tasks as parents fulfill their duties. The Christian journey begins at birth, and Christian formation begins at birth as well. In the early months of a child's life, this formation may simply take the form of loving – truly loving – the child despite its cries for milk, its irrational temper tantrums, its dirty diapers, and its disruption of sleep and life as the parents used to know it. Formation might consist of devoting oneself to the child's needs fully and in joyful servanthood, putting aside one's own needs for a time. This is part of welcoming the child as one would welcome Christ himself. This is truly living out the Christian life and message in a profound way that will affect both the child and the parents as they all undergo a marvelous transformation.

The parent, both when the child is born and as the child matures, serves as a "godbearer" – one who welcomes Christ by welcoming the child, who nurtures the child as if Christ himself had come into the household, who takes the child into the world and thus takes the natural spirituality and joy of the child into the community as a gift from God. Christian formation is, thus, three-fold. The child is formed; the parents are formed as they mature and strive towards joyful servanthood and stewardship; the community is formed as it experiences a new human being with new gifts and joy and makes way for an ever-growing and ever-changing Christian community.

As the child grows, Christian formation efforts might mature as well. Discipline is not just a child rearing technique; discipline is part of Christian formation as well. Children are born with only their own basic needs in mind. By the time they are adults, and especially the Christian adults we hope they will become, children should be able to see themselves as joyful servants themselves, able and willing to take on the Baptismal Covenants of seeking and serving Christ in all persons, loving their neighbors as themselves, striving for justice and peace, and respecting the dignity of every human being.[109]

The process of a child evolving from a screaming and self-centered infant to a mature adult who can actually understand this covenant, choose to live it, and actually live it does not happen in the course of a Sunday School class. This process takes a lifetime and requires the constant diligence and vigilance of parents and others who form the child's community – those who care to take the time and effort necessary to mold the child, with God's help, on a daily basis and in everyday situations. This is not an easy task, nor one to be taken lightly.

This is also a task and a process that cannot and should not be delegated in full to teachers or child care workers. This type of Christian formation and parenting – the day- to-day molding of a child's character – requires constant vigilance and attention to the multitude of "teachable moments" that take place among the everyday living of life. A child might learn respect for others by observing the way his or her parent deals with other people at the grocery store, when answering the front door, when dealing with relatives, friends and neighbors as they share their turmoils, their joys, their crises, their fears. The child is watching, and learning. This richness of experiential learning cannot be taken into the classroom and cannot be presented to the child within the limited scope of a Christian education program or other institutional environment.

On the other hand, learning must also be intentional at times. A child who regularly attends worship services and parish social events will indeed "learn" much of what the Christian life and message is about from observing others and from experiencing a place in the faith community. However, the child needs to learn the basic Bible stories and the basic elements of the liturgy in an intentional manner.

The Gospel as read and preached in the parish during the worship service is generally not presented in an age appropriate way for toddlers and small children (assuming a children's chapel or children's homily is not available). Generally, no visual or kinesthetic aids are available to assist the child in grasping the story. There are many, many distractions in a room full of adults, and it is likely that the Gospel and other scripture lessons soar way over the heads of most children – assuming they are in the service at all and are not stuck in the church nursery. We also do not generally take time during the service itself to explain to children (or anyone else) what the chalice and paten are for, why we might mix water with the wine, why the priest is holding bread up in the air, and why everyone is given a piece of bread and a sip of wine when they go up to the altar rail.

Parents could present the stories of the Bible to their children in an age appropriate way, through the use of age appropriate Bible story books with scriptural integrity or through other means, such as materials used in *Catechesis of the Good Shepherd* or *Godly Play*. In a perfect world, parents might take time on a regular basis to read the child a story, say prayers, or afford the child some means of having time and space to actively work towards Christian growth.

However, even if parents took the time to, in effect, "homeschool" their children in the Christian life and faith, the child would not get the complete picture. The Christian life and faith are lived in community, not simply in the home and not individually. Families are part of the Body of Christ, and children (along with all adults) should experience growth in community as well as individually, in a format in which they can learn from each other, in which they can share their unique stories and perspectives. The old-fashioned Sunday School and other Christian formation programs for children, therefore, are still as relevant today as they ever were.

*Receiving the Gifts of Teachers*

But who should teach these Christian formation classes for children? If the parents are truly doing a terrific job of nurturing their children in the Christian faith at home and in the world - showing support of their children by helping with school projects and shepherding kids through homework and other after school activities - they may be too exhausted to also prepare and teach a Christian formation class. Parents also might not have the skills to teach a class of children (as opposed to just one, two or three children), and they might not have the time or training to teach the Bible stories and other basics of the faith in a knowledgeable, intentional, effective way.

The Apostle Paul, in the First Letter to the Corinthians, sets forth a beautiful image of what the faith community is and how it should function – as the Body of Christ.[110] Not every member of the faith community is expected to function as its hands, or its feet, its brain, or its heart, lungs, kidneys, or any other of the many functions that keep the Body alive. Not every member of the faith community is expected or even able to perform the same tasks or ministries. The task of Christian parenting is a function of the Body of Christ. The function of teacher of children is a related but different function. These functions should work hand in hand and support one another.

Paul, in fact, bookends the imagery of the Body of Christ with language that plainly delineates different functions and gifts, including the gift of teaching. In listing gifts of the Spirit in I Corinthians 12:1-11, Paul lists gifts which the ordinary parent may or may not have – the utterance of wisdom, the utterance of knowledge, faith and prophecy – all gifts that a teacher of the Christian faith might have. After the image of the Body of Christ is presented, Paul specifically lists the appointment of teachers in the church as not only leaders, but leaders third in importance only to apostles and prophets, in I Corinthians 12:28.

The rhetorical question is asked in this scripture passage, "Are all teachers?"[111] Paul's implicit answer is "no." The author of the Book of James is more blunt, saying, "[n]ot many of you should be teachers, my brothers and sisters, for you know that we who teach will be judged with greater strictness."[112] Clearly, there is strong scriptural basis for the role of teacher as that which not everyone in the church should or can undertake.

The role of teacher is a role utilizing special gifts and talents for the essential task of Christian formation and the continuation of the Christian tradition. The role of teacher is one of special knowledge and skills, of having something important to say and techniques with which to get the message across to children in a meaningful way which they will pay attention to, understand, and apply in their own lives. Not every parent or parishioner has a "knack" with children, particularly in a group setting. Many parents do not have a clue of how to even get a room full of children to sit still and listen to them for more than two seconds. Many parents do not have the skills with which to take very complicated theological concepts (such as redemption, resurrection, servanthood, miracles, anemnesis) and present them in a way that those under the age of twelve can even begin to understand.

There are those members of the Body of Christ who do have these gifts and are willing to share them with children. Some members of the Body of Christ are able to lead three year olds in sitting in a state of silence and meditation for several minutes. Some members of the Body of Christ are able to present to children the concept of bringing the story of the Last Supper into our present lives as we celebrate Eucharist. Some members of the Body of Christ are able to recognize that a particular child may "get" a concept better by working with his hands or by drawing a picture than by participating in an auditory discussion. Some members of the Body of Christ may have the gift of lending a listening ear to a small child and discussing deep theological concerns that the parent may not be equipped to discuss, for whatever reason.

The Church, in serving as the Body of Christ, needs to recognize these skills and talents, accept them, and utilize them as the precious gifts from God that they are. To do otherwise would be poor stewardship of great magnitude, wasting spiritual gifts of tremendous importance to children and to the Church as a whole.

The entire structure of Christian education for children generally does not recognize the role of those having the spiritual gifts of teachers. Though some gifted teachers are teaching our children in Christian formation classes, in parishes, the task of teaching is to be done in the teacher's spare time, on the weekend, and in addition to that person's profession and parental duties. Teaching in the church has become something we ask people to do as an ancillary activity, not as something they would do "professionally," with time spent adequately preparing for classes and gathering needed materials, with opportunities to grow spiritually and to develop needed skills and education.

The church has gone far, far astray from the role of teachers in scripture and in the early church. The church has been a poor steward of the gifts of teaching among us. Budgets do not include salaries for really terrific teachers and typically do not even cover the costs of the materials and facilities they need. Those called to the ministry of teaching in the church do not have professional, paid job opportunities available to them and may not be able to fulfill their calling at all if they must work at other jobs to pay the bills. Some churches may not even utter the words "thank you" to those called to this ministry and who practice their calling as a labor of love at personal sacrifice.

These failures to honor and support those called to the ministry of teaching have become millstones around the neck of the Body of Christ, pulling many children down into poor or nonexistent programs of Christian formation. The inadequacies of the past have left their own parents incapable of teaching them as well. The Church, more than ever before, needs to identify anew the role of teacher, hold it up as important, and make good stewardship of those who have gifts to give and talents to share.

*Pointing Out the Green Pastures*

In the Episcopal Church, there is no official guidance for Christian educators (professional or otherwise) as to choice of curriculum, training needed, choice of subject matter, or anything else. Currently, every parish in the church must come up with its own plan, and they can do anything they want. Even diocesan or provincial guidance is minimal or non-existent in many areas of the country. A handful of curricula and programs are widely used in the church, but none of these is supported financially by the national church, and none of them – even the quality programs – are promoted or encouraged in any way. A few parishes in the Episcopal Church have high quality, effective and popular Christian education programs; many parishes have very low quality programs, if they have any programs at all.

The current "do whatever you want" policy may

have had a place in past years, when the only voices heard in the Church may have been those of white males with clerical collars. Other voices did indeed need to be heard. Opening the door for many voices to be heard in the development of Christian education curriculum was probably a good experiment in past years, allowing new curriculum designers to have a chance to offer new and exciting means of "doing" Christian formation. This policy might support the theology that all people of faith have something important to say.

However, this policy does not support an overriding theology of every member of the Body of Christ having different gifts. Nor does this policy support the theology of some members of the faith community being called to serve in specific leadership roles, namely those of apostle, prophet, and teacher.

Not every member of the faith community is a brain cell; not every member of the faith community has the gifts, skills, talent or education to write curriculum or to develop sound policies which are in line with Anglican tradition and doctrine. The tradition of the church and the theology of Anglicanism has always been that there are indeed those members of the faith community who should take leadership positions, who should point the way to a new vision of what the faith community might become, who have the skills and the leadership to build up the church and make it a stronger Body of Christ. By continuing on a path of "everybody do their own thing," the church is not only ignoring strong, theologically sound tradition but also exercising poor stewardship of gifted individuals.

This theology of having strong leadership was developed at a time when the Church was young and needed knowledgeable people of faith who had the skills to teach and a talent for building up their faith communities. That era is upon us again. The Church can no longer afford to be in "maintenance" mode. As Christianity enters a new post-Christendom era where adults in our community may not even know anything about the church, do not know the basics of the Christian faith and are in no position to teach their children about the faith, the critical teaching ministry of the church cannot function without the leadership of those who do know and understand the faith, live it, and have leadership skills and the talents to develop ways in which to share anew what it means to be a Christian.

Jesus' primary occupation was as a teacher.[113] The ministry of teaching was important in Jesus' ministry and tremendously important in the early days of the church. To be faithful to its call and tradition, the church might well reclaim this important ministry of teaching. Before the church can nurture the faithful to serve in soup kitchens and in homeless shelters, on altar guilds and on vestries, as teachers of children and as lay ministers to the sick and the needy, the faithful need to understand what Christianity is about and what it means to live one's life as a Christian in the world. Otherwise, these ministries may further decline into mere "do-gooding" or cease to function at all. The church might serve again as a *sensus fidelium*,[114] a sense of the faith and sense of how this faith might be lived out in the world, rather than merely assuming that parishioners in the pews (not to mention those in society who never darken the church's doors) already embrace the Christian life and message.

Before this task can be carried out on the parish level and on a widespread basis in the church, leadership will be needed to first make the teaching ministry of the church a priority again and then to equip teachers (lay and ordained) to teach and teach well. The bishops, in their roles as shepherds of the church, might greatly enhance the ministry of the church by pointing out greener pastures where the teaching ministry of the church might be reclaimed and by truly shepherding the flock in the direction of these pastures. If the church continues its policy of "anybody doing anything they want," the shepherds are, in effect, letting the sheep wander at will. Some will find green pastures and the still waters by themselves. Others will wander off and get seriously lost. Others may be lost for good. Some may become malnourished or injured.

A Good Shepherd, however, cares whether the sheep are healthy and actively undertakes to feed them. A Good Shepherd will be vigilant in making sure all the sheep stay together, stay within certain boundaries, do not go wandering off alone where they can get into trouble, and do indeed find the pasture lands and the water they need to sustain themselves. A Good Shepherd keeps the wolves away and fends off danger. A Good Shepherd might employ sheepdogs and helpers when the flock is large and he or she needs help with managing or feeding the flock.

In feeding their own flocks, the bishops of the church might see that their flocks are fed by providing teachers, curriculum, time, and space for parishioners to grow in their faith and ministry in ways they will find satisfying to their hunger. Bishops might designate certain standards and requirements for high quality programs and catechists. Bishops might employ the assistance of trained professionals who might assist with these tasks and provide resources to priests, parishes, lay teachers, and parishioners. True apostles might be called to truly build up the teaching ministry of the church. Modern day prophets might be asked to point to a new vision of what the church might become and how the church might achieve this vision.

Christian Nurture in the Twenty-First Century

A NEW AND RENEWED VISION

FOR CHRISTIAN FORMATION

CHAPTER FOUR

If the Church hopes to continue its message and ministry in the twenty-first century, Christian formation of children is critical. The current declining numbers of adults attending church is not a phenomenon that developed overnight. Neither is the clergy shortage currently faced by many denomination an overnight event. If the Church wants people in its pews as adults and if the Church hopes to have priests and other leaders, the Church needs to nurture these people as infants, as toddlers, as school age children and as teenagers. The current models for doing so, however, are not working.

A huge gap exists in Christian education literature in setting the direction towards much needed reforms. Most Christian bookstores offer books which are purely practical in nature, usually along the lines of "cute ideas to boost Sunday School attendance." While these books are surely well-intentioned, they do not address the root challenges to Christian education: the time crunch faced by most parents, the dreadful lack of knowledge and preparation on the part of most teachers, and the failure of parents to see that they have a role in their own children's Christian formation. More importantly, books such as these are more in the vein of marketing ideas, rather than theological ideas that should be the driving forces in a Christian formation program.

On the other hand, there are theorists, many of them from the academic community, who will paint very big pictures for a new vision of Christian education. These theorists might suggest that we look at "curriculum" not simply as a teacher's guide but as *koinonia, leiturgia, diakonia, kerygma* and *didache*.[115] A recently published book that purported to set a vision for Christian education in the third millennium offered articles by learned scholars on such topics as sacramental teaching, congregational education, cross-disciplinary thinking, transformative learning, and other very abstract topics.[116] This publication featured many thoughtful articles by well-known, respected authors with many credentials. Yet none of these articles offered advice for the average Director of Christian Education out in the field to actually provide a quality and theologically sound Christian formation program for children.

Theology needs to be linked with practicalities and current realities. Theology needs to ask and answer the questions arising in everyday parish life, such as: who should be teaching children, when and where should Christian formation be taking place, and who should set the direction of Christian nurture and formation? Once the theology of Christian nurture is set and these questions asked and answered, the programs and approaches needed by the Church fall into place.

*Parents As Primary Christian Educators*

Scripture, theology, and the tradition of the Church are clear – parents have always been considered the primary Christian educators of their own children. What then does this mean for the parent and the parish in the current reality? This means, quite simply, the parents are responsible for the Christian formation of their own children. The church is not obligated to provide all the Christian education a child will need. The Church *cannot* provide all the Christian education a child will need. Christianity is lived and learned in the home and out in the world, not simply within the confines of a classroom for one hour on Sunday morning.

The parent is the child's guide and teacher as the child grows in the home and in the world, especially during the early years of a child's life. The child learns how to treat other people, how to spend one's time, how to make good stewardship of one's gifts and blessings, and how to relate to God on a daily basis – all by watching parents and other adults in his world. Patterns for daily life are set from the beginning, before the child is even ready for a formal Sunday School class. The most profound, most long-lasting, and most effective means of teaching a child (or perhaps anyone else) the Christian faith is by demonstrating it by one's actions. Jesus himself did not teach in formal "classes." Jesus taught out in the world, in the midst of daily life, using "teachable moments" he encountered along the way.

Much of this teaching will be done with pre-school aged children not typically served by church school programs, as the patterns of children's lives and behavior are "set" at an early age.[117] Even if professional teachers are available later on to teach children in an intentional way, the material and presentations they make to the children must be reinforced and lived in the home and in the world if they are to do any good at all. If the child sees and experiences something other than the lived Christian faith at home, in school, and in other parts of her world, the Christian message will at best be subordinated to simply a quaint and idealistic way of living one's life. More likely, the message presented in formal church teachings will get lost in the shuffle or rejected.

In homes where the child is raised by mature adults of faith, the child also needs the intentionality of individual tutoring and modeling by her parents. The parents of the child know their child better than any other adult (or should). The family continually acts as a teaching team, using a mixture of teaching methods geared towards the needs, interests, and individual means of learning for each child.[118] All children will have existential and theological questions. These questions will likely arise in daily life, outside any institutions, as the child deals with issues of life and death, justice and injustice, gifts and burdens to bear. The parents are the adults the child will likely approach to discuss these often very personal and intimate issues. The child may indeed go to a Christian formation teacher with such questions. But the teacher may or may not have the time and space with which to address such questions and have a thorough discussion with the child.

The role of parent as primary Christian educator is a role that cannot be shirked or delegated solely to teachers if children are to truly grow up understanding and living the Christian faith. The Church must first underscore the duty of parents to take the lead in their own children's Christian formation. The Church must also equip the parents themselves to themselves understand and live the faith.

*Teach the Adults*

In providing Christian nurture of children, of those it hopes will become its mature adults of faith and leaders, the Church must first teach the teachers.[119] As a first step in leading new parents towards Christian nurture of their own children, parents should be made explicitly and continually aware of the scriptural, theological, and traditional roles of parents as primary Christian educators. Baptism is not just a social rite of passage. Baptism means something, and the vows the parents make mean something.

As apostles, as teachers, and as priests baptizing infants and children, the clergy should make parents abundantly aware of this aspect of their Baptismal vows. This teaching might take the form of discussions with each couple presenting a child for Baptism. This teaching might take the form of a more formal "class" which each parent might be required to undergo before their child is baptized. This teaching might also take the form of mature Christians demonstrating Christian parenting to other parents.

After Baptism, this message must be highlighted and preached from time to time. Parents should also be reminded often and clearly of their own duties in living out the Baptismal Covenant and in raising their children in working towards fulfilling these covenants as adults. This is what the church is about. This is the curriculum. If the church does not take these teachings and tasks seriously itself, it cannot expect much more than nominal Christian parenting on the part of the adults.

Much of the "teaching" of this curriculum by the parents with their children will be done on a day to day basis, in the home and as the parents take their children out into the world. Parents will need guidance in presenting to their children concepts such as: continuing in the apostles' teaching and fellowship, persevering in resisting evil and repenting and returning to the Lord, proclaiming by word and example the Good News of God in Christ, seeking and serving Christ in all persons, and striving for justice and peace among all people.

Much of this "teaching" of the adults might be done informally, by the very actions of the church itself - by what it engages in, by what it does not engage in, and the very ethos of how it operates. The church then serves very specifically and intentionally as a *sensus fidelium*,[120] a sense of the faithful and the true Christian message among competing secular forces. If, for instance, lack of time and stresses arising from time constraints is an issue for millions of people, the church could certainly connect with many disillusioned Christians by facing the issue head-on and by modeling an alternative life-style to parents of young children. Instead of competing with the secular world in demanding time, efforts, and energies from our parishioners[121] that they do not have, the church might first tend to their needs for quiet retreat, for a nutritious meal, for a sense of rootedness[122] in an every changing and ever transient world.

If parents of young children seek guidance in raising their children in the moral life, the church certainly has a role to play in the development of morality and many important concepts and messages to give them, if only the church will reclaim this role in parents' life. Morality and law in America were founded upon Judeo-Christian principles, and by holding up the roots of these concepts – loving one's neighbor as one's self, justice, mercy, acting in community – churches might model to parents the guidelines they so sorely need and now seem to want.

Will the church lose people by taking seriously these covenants and the teaching of them to children? Yes. The church will lose those who come into the church merely seeking in Baptism a social rite of passage and excuse for a nice party. Yet the church might also find that it has a message and a mission that young parents very much *want* to hear and a theology of child rearing that is very much in tune with the young adults raising small children in this new millennium – theology practiced out in the world.

American culture appears on the brink of a downscaling of extracurricular events in children's lives and the overscheduling and frantic shuttling all over town that many families experience. A front page headline in *USA Today* proclaimed, "More Americans put families ahead of work" and chronicled the efforts of parents to take more time off to spend with their children.[123] Another feature article profiled organized efforts by communities in several parts of the United States to encourage families to simply stay at home and be together for simple activities they can do together.[124]

These trends, along with a yearning of parents to better instill values and morality into their children,[125] are completely compatible with the theology and practical ramifications of parents as the primary Christian educators of their own children. If parents are to use precious "teachable moments" to share the Christian faith with their children, they will indeed need time spent together and time off from extracurricular activities – including overburdening church activities. If the church truly wants parents to nurture their children in the faith, churches might set as their own priorities encouraging, empowering and affording families the gift of time spent together - whether that time is spent in doing outreach projects together, learning scripture together, or spending time at home.

As the church asks parents to spend more time with their own children, churches may need to appreciate that these adults might need to shift, for a time, their volunteer time and efforts to children's ministries and away from ministries they may have been engaged in before their children came along. Parents might be encouraged and allowed to put other obligations aside for a time to focus on the Christian formation and activities of their own children at this stage of their lives – "life-stage appropriate" volunteer opportunities. Better yet, parishes might better include children in outreach activities, worship services, and other church functions to "teach" them the role and mission of the church in a wonderfully experiential way.

*Teach the Basics*

If parents are indeed to function as primary Christian educators of their own children, where does this leave the institutional church as a teaching body that seeks to teach adults in a formal, intentional way? In order to nurture adults in becoming the mature persons of faith needed to raise its next generation, the church needs very desperately to focus on the basics.

The typical model in the Episcopal Church is the "adult forum," which typically consists of series of special interest topics, sometimes led by invited guest speakers, sometimes led by laypersons who may or may not have theological training, and sometimes based primarily upon the interests of the clergy at the time. The adult forum method was never intended to function as the sole vehicle of Christian education for adults.[126] Instead, the Sunday morning format was intended to simply supplement the Christian education that had already occurred in childhood, in the community, and even in public schools.[127] It is assumed, by presenting these special interest topics, that adults already know the basics.

Adults do not already know the basics. Relying on special interest topics in an adult forum format is akin to skipping to dessert before the meat, potatoes, and vegetables have been served. Parishes need to first teach basic Old Testament, New Testament, Church History, Sacraments, and other meat and potatoes type courses. While these course might not seem glamorous, churches might likely find that young adults hunger for the lessons they never got as children (in meager or non-existent Sunday Schools) or because they simply did not go to church as children. Churches might also find that after they do teach the basics, their parishioners might be more conscious of a sense of mission within the church, more equipped to serve as leaders and volunteers within the church and the community, and much more conscientious and able teachers of their children and others.

The church, in effect, needs to reclaim the programs and methodology of the early church: teach what the Christian life is like, teach the scriptures, instruct in the sacraments. New Christians and nominal Christians might be allowed the time and guidance to go through a full process of truly growing in faith and growing as Christians. Then, they might serve as teachers guiding their own children in the faith.

The church might also be intentional in guiding parents as the primary Christian educators of their own children by providing resources and classes for equipping parents in serving out their responsibilities as Christian parents. Church nurseries might serve as resource labs to demonstrate the use of age appropriate and scripturally sound Bible stories with very small children. Catechists or clergy might also take time to demonstrate to parents prayer and meditative time with small children.

A much needed resource that liturgical churches might provide to their parishioners are books to be read with and by children. Many resources available at bookstores – even Christian bookstores – do not have scriptural integrity (by having the three magi appear at the stable on the night Jesus is born, for instance[128]) or do not square with Anglican doctrine (by stating that the Roman Catholic church is the one true church, for instance, or by putting too much emphasis on children's sinfulness, as might be the case in more fundamentalist resources). If parents are being asked to serve as primary

Christian educators of their children, they will need age appropriate resources to use at home. Even the most conscientious parent needs help in presenting Bible stories in an engaging manner. The Evangelical churches do a great job of putting money into church-owned publishing companies and bookstores that put resources into the hands of the average parent in the suburbs. If the Episcopal Church wants children to learn Christianity from an Anglican perspective, it will need to do more to put Anglican resources in their hands and in an affordable, accessible and engaging format.

The church might also provide more resources for the parents themselves by way of books or the internet. Even the busiest of parents has time to read a book from time to time. Books can be taken anywhere and read anywhere – while waiting for children on the soccer field or in the gymnastics facility, while traveling on a plane on the way to a business meeting – and can succinctly "teach" parents about raising children in the Christian faith. Instead of asking parents to rely solely on secular child-raising texts, the church might consider providing parents with its own message, written with respect to Christian principles. The Church might consider making its message relevant to issues adults deal with every day and more actively disseminating that message.

Christianity exists in a new world of far-reaching technologies that can put the message of Christianity in the hands of those willing to hear it quickly and relatively inexpensively. The teaching ministry of the church has never had such opportunity for quality mission work – through websites, email, and other telecommunications - if only the church will seize upon these opportunities and use them.

However, a major element of "teaching" the Christian life and faith is the human element of learning from each other in community. Even if quality resources were available, even if parents were very well equipped themselves to teach their own children the Christian message, people of all ages still need to be in Christian community together, to truly continue in the apostles' teaching *and fellowship*.

If parents are the primary Christian educators of their own children, does that mean we disband the Sunday School system? Not at all. Children need to learn what it means to be part of a Christian community in an age appropriate manner and in ways they find engaging and understandable. Christian education in community is a vital element of each child's Christian formation.

With parents as primarily Christian educators of their own children, we do not do away with formal

Christian formation classes. We revitalize them.

*New Models of "Sunday School"*

As a new model of providing Sunday morning Christian education in accordance with the theology of parents as primary Christian educators, parents might be asked to form cooperatives among themselves to accomplish this task. If all parents have the responsibility to teach the basics of the faith, this task should not be dumped on only one or two parents. Parents and parishes might also see other benefits of bringing together a number of parents to work together. Aside from being intentional about learning and teaching the basics of the faith, these parents might also form community among themselves, get to know each other well, share their gifts in Christian fellowship, and model Christian community for their children.

Parents could be asked to share their particular gifts and do what they reasonably can do. If one particular parent is not adept in telling a Bible story and leading a group discussion among children, another parent might take on this responsibility and let others provide snacks, lead art and crafts activities, or supervise children in fellowship time on the playground. All parents have different gifts and talents, and no one parent should be expected to take on the responsibility of leading children in a Christian education class alone. If parents pull together and share in providing a formation experience for a group of children, the whole could truly be greater than the sum of the parts – and certainly greater than the results of asking one or two already stressed and busy parents to do it by themselves.

The role of Christian education directors might then shift to supporting such "co-ops" by calling organizational meetings, suggesting ways of dividing up responsibilities, helping parents to identify their own gifts and contributions, and by suggesting curriculum resources which are in line with Anglican doctrine, have scriptural integrity, and which the parents might reasonably be able to do for their children. Christian education directors would then be free to train parents of smaller children, teach adult offerings, provide information on available resources to parents and others, or take on other tasks requiring professional training and skills.

Parent cooperatives – which may in fact already exist in small parishes – do not by any means have to happen only on Sunday mornings and only while concurrent adult classes are taking place. Christian formation takes place out in the world or in the home as much or more as it does in the church building. Families might agree to meet after school, at their homes, on a weeknight, on Saturday, on Sunday afternoon, or at some other time or place. In fact, a greater sense of community might be facilitated by joining Christian formation with a group dinner, snacks, or other social occasion – literally, continuing in the apostles' *teaching and fellowship*. Parents might find that they are more able to relax and simply get to know each other at times other than Sunday morning, a time when parents of small children are usually rushed to get to the worship service, sleepy from Saturday activities, and when the many activities taking place on a typical Sunday in the parish are just too much for young children.

Neither do such classes have to take place each and every Sunday. In order to prevent burn-out and honor the concept of Sabbath, parishes might consider planning breaks in the program year to coincide with school breaks or long weekends. Parishes might also consider offering programs on Wednesday nights or at other times when parents are not as rushed and will not be asked to give up part of their "down time" on Saturday in order to prepare for a class. Parishes might also look at summer programs or other times when families are looking for something to do together, instead of trying to compete against already too-full schedules. Consistency in learning and spiritual disciplines are good things, but if churches try to have programs just to have programs, they risk losing enthusiasm for these programs.

Adult offerings, too, do not have to be confined to Sunday mornings and only within the space of an hour. In fact, the best adult programs currently available –those which are well designed, comprehensive, and effective in assisting adults in growing in faith, such as the Anglican *Alpha* and *EFM* and the Methodist *Disciple* programs – are all designed to take place over at least a two hour period and at a time other than Sunday morning.

Christian formation is not a process that can be rushed or given short shrift. If adults truly want to grow in faith, they will need to make time and space in their schedules for Christian formation, as will those leading and teaching them. We cannot expect quality Christian formation to happen for parishioners of any age if adult teachers never get to attend adult offerings or are asked to skip classes in order to teach children on a regular basis. True community, among children and the adults leading them, cannot take place unless there is consistency of attendance and commitment of those participating, no matter their age.

*The Case for Professional Catechists*

Despite good intentions of parents who might be both willing and able to provide Christian formation experiences for their own children in the home and despite the importance of informal Christian formation in the home, there may come a time in the life of a parish when the parents just do not have the time or resources to fully carry out the task of Christian education of their children. This is a centuries-old dilemma. In 1524, Martin Luther addressed the "I don't have time" problem of his own culture by identifying the understandable neglect of catechesis in the home by parents who simply had too many other things going on in their lives.[129] Luther's solution, however, was not to berate parents for their neglect and ask them to take on volunteer positions they did not have time to do. His solution was not to simply let the matter go. His solution was Christian formation undertaken by professionals.

*The School Model*

The mechanism for catechesis in Luther's scheme of professional Christian formation was the school. In Reformation Germany, schoolteachers also taught the Bible and the other basics of religion. Even as late as the mid-twentieth century in America, religion was unabashedly taught in the public schools. Then, after United States Supreme Court decisions in 1963 banning teacher-led school prayer and Bible study,[130] American schools lost an important source of formal catechesis that likely will not return to public schools again.

This source of catechesis is still possible, however, in parochial schools. Church –sponsored schools may still actively teach Christianity on a formal, intentional basis and, perhaps as importantly, may provide a Christian ethos for children, teaching the Christian life experientially.[131] Teachers do not have to put their faith on a shelf when they teach and in fact may make their faith part of their teaching. Children may have the experience of having their faith be part of their everyday world, not separated out and only attended to on Sunday morning.

Many of the problems faced are parishes are largely avoided in parochial schools. Children attend their religion classes in parochial schools on a regular, consistent basis. Teachers do not have to face problems of children only attending the religion class sporadically or at the parent's convenience. Both children and parents take the class seriously, because it is a regular part of the curriculum. Teachers are prepared, knowledgeable, and skilled. Perhaps most importantly, children whose parents do not attend church on Sunday morning and who would not otherwise attend any Christian formation classes at all may still be exposed to the message of Christianity.

Every family cannot, however, afford to send their children to Episcopal parochial schools or may not choose this option of education for other reasons. Although the Episcopal Church might do well to provide more parochial schools for its children, in the mold of the Catholic Church, this option is admittedly an expensive one and an alternative not feasible in many locations or for many families. The next most likely candidate for providing professional catechesis, then, is the local parish.

*The Church Model*

When a child is baptized, the parents are not the only people who pledge to provide Christian nurture of him. Every time a child is baptized in the Episcopal Church, the entire congregation vows "to do all in [their] power to support these persons in their life in Christ."[132] This vow could mean many things. At this time, most parishioners likely simply say the words and have never been pressed to examine what this vow might mean for their parish. As a reality, the closest most parishes come to living out this vow is for a handful of parishioners to volunteer to serve as children's ministries volunteers. In some parishes, volunteer-led Christian formation classes or parent cooperatives might work very well. Yet in many other parishes, volunteer efforts and parent efforts simply might not be enough to provide quality Christian formation programs.

The vow to do "all in your power" to support newly baptized persons is by no means limited to efforts by overworked volunteers. "All in your power" could mean for individual parishes and the church as a whole exciting new ways to provide Christian formation experiences to children and others. The beauty of this language is in its unlimited possibilities.

Parishes might consider revitalizing their Christian formation programs by asking trained professionals to lead classes for children. "Professional" catechists have been used in the teaching ministry of the church since the very early days of Christianity. The ministry of professionals who use their particular gifts and talents in service to others is fully in line with scripture. These professionals would be using their particular spiritual gifts and fulfilling their call to a particular ministry.

These professionals might be utilized in a variety of ways. James Michael Lee has proposed a model of Christian formation using professional teachers who would be assisted by paraprofessionals and volunteers.[133] In the Lee model, parish religious education programs would be directed by salaried, professional teachers. They would be assisted by trained assistants. Untrained volunteers with the desire or calling to help with the program would still have a place in this model, but they would take the role of rendering occasional assistance to teachers and their assistants.[134] Lee also acknowledges the role of interns in his model.[135]

While James Michael Lee calls for salaried professionals, in order to show the value of the work of religious education teachers[136], Gabriel Moran has defined "professional" in broader terms. Moran has defined "professional" in the Christian education context as (a) those who feel called to the ministry of teaching, (b) those who are needed to perform certain teaching tasks, (c) those who possess skills and talents needed in the ministry of teaching, and (d) those who take their responsibilities seriously and hold themselves to high standards.[137] Payment of these professionals, in the Moran model, is not the crux of whether of whether a teacher is professional. The mark of a teacher is whether he or she takes his calling and duties seriously.

These two models alone suggest a variety of possibilities for revitalization of parish Christian formation programs. Bolstering the quality of teaching by hiring staff teachers or catechists – on a full or part-time basis – is fully supported both in early church history and in scripture. Since the days of *The Didache*, Christians have been urged to support those who teach the Gospel. Parishes might, in doing all in their power to support the newly baptized, choose to offer an honorarium or salary to those with special skills or training in Christian education and who are following a calling.

At present, laypersons called to teach are usually not given the opportunity to fully develop and share their gifts. Even if a layperson has gifts and talents for teaching in the church and is willing to share those gifts, that person likely has financial responsibilities to meet, a job to hold down, children to raise, and a multitude of other volunteer tasks he or she is asked to do. By offering a paid position – or even by holding up the duties of "catechist" as a serious and defined ministry – we at least give talented teachers the space to develop their gifts, receive needed training, and to better prepare to teach others.

Though the primary educational need faced by most parishes is for teachers of children and youth, professional lay catechists might also be used to provide more comprehensive Christian formation programming for adults as well. With pastoral care duties, worship services to hold, sermons to write, financial issues to tackle, employees to supervise, and a multitude of other duties to perform, the clergy in any given parish will not be able to take the time necessarily to fully carry out the task of adult Christian formation needed in this new era of post-Christendom.

At the same time, many parishes have a number of active retirees, mothers of school-aged children, and others who might make wonderful teachers and, would, with training, be able to more fully focus on time-consuming lesson preparation and program development. Clergy would then be more free to perform tasks that may only be performed by those who are ordained or could more fully step into the role of church administrator and spiritual leader of the ministries of others.

In the Constitution and Canons of the Episcopal Church, there already exists church legislation providing for the licensing by bishops of lay catechists.[138] These catechists would, under this canon, undergo training in scriptures, the Book of Common Prayer, the Hymnal, church history, the doctrine of the church as set forth in the Creeds and the Catechism, and in the methodology of catechesis itself.[139] Lay catechists would then be allowed to train others in preparation for baptism, confirmation, reception, and the reaffirmation of baptismal vows[140] - all the "mile markers" of Christian formation for children and the adults raising them.

With creativity, vision, and energy, professional catechists could be utilized effectively to provide Christian formation opportunities to both large and small parishes. A move towards professional catechists need not leave out small parishes with few resources. In fact, small parishes could be greatly assisted by a move towards professional teachers. Rather than rely solely on the talents of available volunteers within a parish, dioceses could train and employ catechists who would then be available where they are most needed. Small churches could also pool their resources, employing catechists to serve several churches. Dioceses or church co-operatives in cities might also form catechetical schools to serve all children within a geographical location. Parochial schools could offer after-school or summer Christian education programs for those of their denomination who cannot afford the tuition of regular day school.

Any of these possibilities will take leadership, vision, openness to change, and effort. Any of the possibilities will need shepherds to gather the flock and lead them to new and greener pastures.

*Shepherds Needed*

Even if parents are charged with the primarily responsibility of raising their children in the Christian faith, and even if we uphold the gifts and talents of teachers to supplement the Christian nurture of the parents, the parents and the teachers can only do what they are inspired, empowered, and equipped to do. The average parent in the pew might not realize that he or she is primarily responsible for raising a child in the Christian faith. Many parents point fingers at the unpaid, overworked Sunday School teachers to provide their children's religious training without a second thought. The volunteer Sunday School teachers may point their own fingers back at the parents, exasperated at them for bringing their children to formation classes on an irregular basis (or not at all) and for not lifting a finger to support their efforts.

If the task of Christian formation is important, the shepherds of the church - bishops and priests - need to say so. These shepherds might also need assistant shepherds – lay catechists - to assist them in the time-consuming task of providing Christian formation programs, in teaching the parents to teach their own children, in teaching the children themselves. If these laypersons are to be successful in assisting the clergy with the nurture of future generations of Christians, they will need resources and training. Their work will need to be honored and held up as responsibilities worth doing. These laypersons will not be able to function if they are treated as individual cells, working alone. They must be incorporated as part of the Body of Christ, fulfilling their functions in concert with the rest of the Body and fed and nourished by it.

Several individuals and groups within the church – including those involved in *Godly Play*, *Catechesis of the Good Shepherd*, *Alpha*, *EFM*, and *J2A* – have indeed developed without the support or endorsement of the national church. These "smart sheep" have found their own greener pastures by themselves, devising programs that work, training programs for leaders and teachers, guidelines and standards for program consistency, and particular methodologies to be followed by all teachers. These efforts have shown the possibilities of great programming and the difference they can make in people's lives.

However, since the offering of programs such as this is not mandated by any church authorities, the availability of these quality programs is driven by the efforts of individual parishes and priests who see their merit. The larger flock of the Episcopal Church is left wandering, and those parishes and parishioners without strong local leadership and gifted teachers are left with either poor quality or non-existent formation opportunities.

The availability of leadership to drive, support, and implement quality Christian formation opportunities for all will make or break the Christian nurture of future generations. The Body of Christ needs a brain to direct it, to make decisions to benefit it, to consciously enter it into a curriculum of maturing faith for all.

# Christian Nurture in the Twenty-First Century

*Winds of Change*

More broadly needed than sheer leadership in Christian formation is change. Christianity has changed dramatically in recent years. Christian formation will need to change as well to effectively nurture new generations of Christians. Change is at the very heart of Christian formation; the very purpose of Christian education is change for the better, led by the Gospel. If Christian formation is to remain true to itself and to the mission and the faith it serves, Christian formation leaders will themselves seek to ever improve the very nature of the structures of this ministry.

The winds of change can be gentle. The winds of change can also be a thunderstorm. Change is never easy. Yet the thunderstorms that seem so dangerous and threatening ultimately provide the water that replenishes the ground, nourishing the green pastures, nourishing life itself.

## ONWARD AND UPWARD

## CHAPTER FIVE

Exciting, engaging, and effective ways of providing Christian formation opportunities to people of all ages are possible in this new millennium. A level of quality in Christian education not seen in the church in many, many years could return. These new opportunities for Christian formation could instill in Christians a sense of mission and purpose, inspiring and equipping them to renew the church's traditional ministries to the poor and the needy. Nominal Christians, finally finding formation classes that engage them and catechists who have time to discuss their questions and challenge them towards deeper faith, might take on new ministries within the church and in the world and with a passion not seen in a long time.

Yet all these wonderful possibilities take leadership. The vision needs to be identified. The standards need to be set, advocated, and put into place. The revitalization of Christian formation will not take place without change, without new directions to address current realities - while remaining true to scripture and tradition. Just as old buildings become antiquated, sagging, and finally unsafe for further habitation, old ways of providing Christian formation experiences might have to be torn down and new structures built up on solid foundation.[141] Indeed, the crux of the Christian message is the death of the Body of Christ, only to be resurrected and raised up in glorious new form again.

Jesus Christ welcomed children to him, welcoming them into the Christian faith with the simplest of gestures, his open arms. Jesus first modeled Christian nurture of children, and the early church set upon a path of Christian formation of children based on scripture and the early teachings of the apostles. Two thousand years later, children are still born into the Christian faith or to parents not of the Christian faith. The questions facing parents and the church are the same questions posed in the early church and throughout the history of the church:

*Who are the primary Christian educators of children?*

The parents are. As Christianity is lived out in the world and in the home, the parents are a child's role models and first teachers in the actual practice of the Christian faith. A child's natural spirituality can be developed by experiencing the Christian life and message as demonstrated both overtly and in very subtle ways by the parents. The parents must be nurtured towards mature Christianity themselves before they can model the faith to their children.

*What role does the church have in teaching children, and who should be leading children in formal Christian education classes?*

The church is a *sensus fidelium*, a sense of the faithful. The church can inspire parents to raise their children in the Christian faith. The church can engage in a teaching ministry that leads children and adults towards mature Christianity in formal and informal ways. If the parents need help in teaching their children, the church can offer professional catechists or teach the parents to better teach their own children.

*What, then, should the Church be doing to provide nurture and formation of children?*

The Church should reclaim Christian formation as a priority again. Before people may fully and truly live their lives as Christians, they need to know and understand what Christianity is all about. The Church should do all in its power to support persons baptized into the Body of Christ in their life in Christ, whatever their age. The Church should nurture its own growth by fully and wholeheartedly nurturing children in the Christian faith - and by nurturing the parents raising them.

The answers to these questions do not pose easy solutions. But Christian nurture of children is not easy. There is no one sure way to do it. It is a daily process. It will be painful sometimes. We can look to professionals to guide us and assist us. Those professionals themselves will need to be guided and assisted and provided with the time, the space, and the materials with which to work. We as parents will need to undergo ourselves the formation process ourselves, as time consuming and as arduous as that might be, in order to be in a position to model for our children how marvelous, how sublime, how life-giving and how amazingly redemptive and profoundly fulfilling the Christian life might be.

Cynthia Coe

Christian Nurture in the Twenty-First Century

**Essays on Contemporary Christian Formation**

Cynthia Coe

**Re-Thinking "Sunday School"**
**Essays on Children's Christian Formation**

Cynthia Coe

Christian Nurture in the Twenty-First Century

**Why Christian Formation is Important**

Growth is at the crux of the ministry of Christian Formation. As parishes reach out to new members, these newcomers will want to learn about the Christian faith. It is hoped that these newcomers will become vital parts of the community and will eventually take on roles of ministry and leadership themselves. The ministry of Christian Formation, thus, serves as a crucial link between evangelism and all other ministries in the church.

All of us need nurturing in the Christian faith, whether we might be babies still dripping with Baptismal water, children of current members, teenagers with no church home, newcomers to the community, or those struggling with faith issues. The ministry of Christian formation seeks to nourish those seeking faith, help answer difficult questions, help members of the Body of Christ find true community, and lead us all into becoming disciples of Christ and ministers of the Church.

This important ministry is by no means undertaken solely by the clergy or paid Christian education staff. When children or adults are baptized, the priest asks, "will you who witness these vows do all in your power to support these persons in their life in Christ?" It is not a small cadre of Sunday School teachers who run to the font and yell, "I will;" the entire parish responds, "we will." Christian formation is the task of every member of the parish and happens in a variety of ways. Intentional classes and programs are very important in making dedicated space and time for Christian education and for providing a well-balanced curriculum and leadership. After taking part in these experiences, it is hoped that parish members will then go out and be formative, nurturing disciples in other ministries in the parish and in the community.

A Christian Formation ministry might also serve as a model of discipleship and ministry for the rest of the parish. The very best way to "teach" something is to model and demonstrate it. If important work in lay leadership, energy, enthusiasm, and both personal growth and community growth are shown in the ministry of Christian formation, other ministries of the parish will surely take note and might be inspired to revitalize as well.

Christian Nurture in the Twenty-First Century

## "Children's Ministries" –

### What if We Started From Scratch?

Suppose you had never heard the term "Sunday School." Suppose "Sunday School" had remained a highly successful method of teaching literacy skills to children working in British factories on Sunday (their day off) – but had never taken hold in the United States and had eventually become obsolete, even in the UK. What would we then think of as "children's ministries"?

If you heard the term "children ministries" for the very first time, with no preconceptions, you might think this concept meant actually ministering to children with particular needs. You might look at what needs exist among children. You might look at children in need in your own community, in communities beyond your own, and even children in need in other countries or on other continents. You might decide to focus your time and resources on children most in need or children you could feasibly help with resources on hand. You might think about how far your dollars would go to make the most difference in the world.

Looking at "children's ministries" in this way, you might not come up with a program meeting in a room of a suburban parish building for one hour on

Sunday, offering a couple of songs, a Bible story, and a craft. You might end up thinking about children in your local foster care system. You might think about kids living with their moms in your local homeless shelter. You might even think about children who tag along with parents visiting your food pantry to pick up something for dinner.

If you really got to thinking about "children's ministries" as part of work of the global Body of Christ, you might think about those 143 million children in orphanages in Asia, Africa, Eastern Europe, and the Americas. If you really wanted to ministry to children most in need in our world, wouldn't we think of children living without the fundamental love and support of a family as one of our top priorities? Or maybe we would want children in Sub-Saharan Africa to live to adulthood, rather than dying of malaria at the rate of one every minute. This kind of "children's ministry" doesn't look too much like a Sunday morning session on learning the liturgical colors, does it?

In developing what we now know as "Sunday School," Robert Raikes looked around his community of Gloucester, saw a pressing need for education of poor children living in the slums of England, and organized a ministry to address this need. (He was criticized for possibly endangering home-based religious education.)

This ministry of the Anglican Church was undoubtedly one of the most successful ministries in Christianity, working itself out of a job and replaced by state funded education for all children in England and much of the Americas and Europe. But that was the 18$^{th}$ century. This is the 21$^{st}$ century. If we, like Robert Raikes, approached "children's ministries" by looking around our communities, addressing real and pressing needs we saw around us, and focused the Church's time and resources on these needs, what could we as the Body of Christ accomplish in our own time?

## Beyond Sunday School:

## A Five Pointed Star

## of Children's Christian Formation

Christian formation is in the process of huge change. Sunday School - which was originally started as a means of literacy training for children living in the slums of 18th century England – is waning as a means of formation. Attendance continues to drop, and smaller parishes find it increasingly difficult to provide any formal formation program at all.

The upside is that we are now able to look at new and likely more effective ways of forming children in the Christian faith. One method might work best for some families; another method might work better for others. Realistically, most families who have an interest in planting the seeds of lifelong faith in their children and teens will likely utilize more than one method of formation in this new 21st century.

This is a preliminary assessment, but it's looking like these five venues of formation will nurture children in the Christian faith in coming years:

***Parishes***: a number of parishes – particularly larger parishes – will continue to provide lively, quality Sunday School or weeknight/afternoon programs.

***Schools***: Episcopal schools are providing terrific religious education classes, taught by professionals, with chapel attendance a vital part of school life

***Home Life***: As weekends get busier and busier, parents may increasingly turn to books, prayers, and other at-home devotions to both teach children basic Bible stories and concepts, along with practical examples of a life lived in faith. I would love to see more tools available in the Episcopal tradition for parents to use with their own children. Many parents read with their children every night before bedtime, and schools require daily reading by children as well. If quality, affordable resources were available and publicized, at-home formation could be huge. (And you get the added bonus of being able to have conversations one-on-one with children, daily if you want.)

***Media***: For better or for worse, children and teens watch a heck of a lot of movies and television programs, both online and off. Whether we like it or not, the media plays a hugely formative role in what children and teens think about. As a church, we would be wise to make relevant, interesting, well-done videos and other mass media resources and place them where they can be found and shared.

***Camps and Summer Programs***: Parents may not have the wherewithal to get kids to Sunday School early Sunday mornings, but a week during the summer is a whole different matter. What parent isn't looking for a quality program during the summer? Do the math, and a week at a summer church camp can provide more formative time spent with a faith community than a Sunday morning only formation experience. Camps and VBS programs create memorable, in-depth formation programs, along with a sense of community for both regular church-going kids and those whose parents may not attend church regularly.

Do children need to participate in ALL these types of formational activities? My own opinion as a busy mom of 3 kids is…no. In my very humble opinion, taking part in 2 or maybe 3 of these formational activities would be ideal. Attending all 5 types of activities might be overdoing it. We all learn in different ways and from different sources. As leaders of formation programs, we may need to leave it up to the Holy Spirit to direct each child (and adult) to the formational experience that will best meet that individual where they are.

## Catechesis of the Good Shepherd and Godly Play:

## What are the Differences, and Do They Matter?

Years ago, as a novice to children's Christian education and a first year student in Virginia Theological Seminary's master's degree program in Christian education, I dropped a file folder of papers and got them hopelessly out of order. I frowned, unable at a glance to figure out which Sunday school lay-out map pictured a Catechesis of the Good Shepherd atrium and which pictured a Godly Play classroom. I couldn't, at a glance, tell the difference. A few months later, after beginning training in Level One Catechesis and completing an intensive weekend training course in Godly Play, I could indeed tell the difference and even give a synopsis of the two programs to interested parents and clergy. But I am still reminded that at first glance and to most people looking at the programs for the first time, the programs are remarkably similar.

Both programs are offspring of Maria Montessori's work among impoverished children in Italy at the beginning of the twentieth century. Both feature elements of a "prepared environment" of hands-on materials with which children may freely explore scripture and theological concepts. Both emphasize quiet listening to God. Both put high value on the child's ability to experience the work of the Holy Spirit on his or her own.

Perhaps as importantly, both Catechesis and Godly Play are in the business of providing excellent Christian formation opportunities for children in a well thought-out manner. Designers and trainers of both programs have paid careful attention to age-appropriateness, scriptural integrity, and theological content. In my observations, excellent, dedicated teachers who are wonderful ministers to children are drawn and are actively working in both programs.

*Teacher Training – What are the Goals?*

While both programs provide excellent Christian formation for children, they arrive at this point by two very different routes. Catechesis requires teachers ("catechists") to attend 90+ hours of training to become certified in Level 1 (for 3-5 year olds), then further 90+ hour courses for Levels 2 and 3. These training courses are typically conducted through weekend retreats over a two year period. Catechesis training includes lectures and meditations aimed at giving Catechists a very rich grounding in the material presented. In my observations, many people who enthusiastically sign up for these very lengthy training courses say they are looking for a Christian formation experience for themselves as much as they are looking to work with children.

In my mind, Godly Play is more of a skills-based training. The basics of the Montessori method are presented, along with the general theological and methodological bases of the program. However, the beauty of Godly Play is in its very hands-on emphasis on giving prospective teachers actual experience and practice in giving presentations to children and in actually using the materials with their own hands. Trainees are sent out in small groups to study the presentation, work with the materials, and practice giving the presentations. Those who complete the weekend can go back home with several presentations soundly under their belts. The training is very positive, affirming, and builds great confidence in the prospective teacher. It is not necessarily a Christian formation experience for adults (although I have to say I gained many personal spiritual insights in working with blank pieces of paper and crayons myself in the training). Godly Play training is wonderful for those who may have already taken Bible studies, EFM or other adult Christian formation studies and mostly want to learn the specific methodology of Montessori-based formation.

Thus, the training experiences of the two programs are, in my mind, like comparing the proverbial apple and orange. Many look to Catechesis for a full adult formation experience (whether it was designed as such or not). Godly Play assumes participants already are well versed in the basics of the Christian faith and scripture (or perhaps invites those aren't into further adult studies).

Is there a common ground of shared concerns and practical challenges? In my experience, it is becoming increasingly difficult to recruit adults willing to take the 90+ hour course required to become a catechist. Looking around at the parents of children in my atrium at Church of the Ascension in Knoxville this past year, most of the parents are professionals. Even if these parents (many of them women taking a break from careers to raise small children) were to sign up for a lengthy training course, they would almost certainly move on to other ministries or volunteer jobs or exclusively paying jobs after their children start school. Realistically, the one weekend course offered by Godly Play is about the most they will attend.

Does this mean Catechesis is entirely out of bounds for most volunteers? Not necessarily. Parents continue to be interested in "helping." I can't help wondering if an "assistant" certification, focused on skills rather than theology, and offered within a do-able time period (like the Godly Play weekend trainings) might help Catechesis continue into the future.

Time is indeed of the essence when administrators, clergy, and Christian education committees make decisions as to which children's Christian formation curriculum they choose. This element of time and what is realistically "do-able" is, in my opinion, at the crux of Jerome Berryman's revisions to Catechesis as manifested in Godly Play. Most Episcopal parishes offer a one hour block of time on Sunday morning for children's Christian formation. Catechesis, I understand, was designed for a two hour block of time, not necessarily on Sunday morning.

This element of time constraint is critical in understanding why a particular parish might choose Godly Play over Catechesis. The time required for teacher training is one major element. Another major element is the time and effort required to procure the materials used in the classroom or atrium. Most of Catechesis materials must be handmade and custom made; Godly Play materials may be ordered over the internet. While the materials used in Catechesis tend to be beautiful products of loving and heart-felt labor, the reality is that many typical parishes just can't pull off the materials-making. As a level two catechist at a typical medium sized parish in the Knoxville suburbs, I struggled to teach an atrium with only half the needed materials. It was a miserable experience, and the program was eventually discontinued.

Personally, I just don't have the skills to make materials, and I have gleefully ordered materials from Godly Play that are also beautiful, well made, and ready for me to use. It's a stewardship issue for me – my gifts and talents are in teaching and ministering to kids, not in carpentry. I am absolutely fine in someone else using their own gifts and talents to make the materials and getting paid for their labors. Many in the church do get paid fair salaries for their efforts!

Does this mean that Catechesis will slowly but surely get snuffed out by an American culture of "not enough time" and not enough workers in the vineyard? Maybe not. Catechesis, as I've experienced it, works best when it is presented as designed - in a two hour block with trained catechists, proper materials, and kids arriving in comfortable play clothes, brought by parents who really and truly want them to be there. This scenario might not necessarily be the same as a typical parish Sunday morning Sunday School offering.

In fact, in Knoxville, the programs that have recently thrived have been the programs offered outside the Sunday morning time block and even outside of the parish building. One home-based Catechesis atrium attracted more children than the Sunday morning parish program. In the past, weekday morning and weekday afternoon programs at my parish were enthusiastically attended, and there was never a lack of trained and available catechists.

More importantly, these non-Sunday morning programs reached children who really and truly needed them. In one weekday two-hour program, one child's parent had just passed away, another child's parent was diagnosed with cancer, and yet another child's father was about to head off to combat duty overseas. The two hour block, guided by two experienced children's ministers, gave us an opportunity to minister to these children in a quiet, spiritual retreat atmosphere using the longer period of time we really needed. After teaching this particular atrium, the Sunday morning program felt very, very rushed to me.

Catechesis "outside the box" of the typical Sunday morning format also opens up the door to ecumenical offerings, creating opportunities for both resource sharing and theological sharing. I was continually amazed at the number of denominations represented in training courses in Knoxville. Participants from Methodist, Orthodox, and even Evangelical churches joined Episcopalians and Roman Catholics in community centered around Catechesis. In this respect, Catechesis might serve best when it is outside just one denomination.

*Anglican vs. Roman Catholic – Does it Matter?*

Does it matter to Episcopal parishes seeking quality children's Christian formation whether the program is Anglican or Roman Catholic in origin and design? While Catechesis has a wonderful ecumenical following, those selecting one curriculum over the other do look at the underlying theology of a program or curriculum. For instance, the designers of the *Episcopal Children's Curriculum* very consciously make sure the theology and practice of the Book of Common Prayer is reflected in the curriculum. Generally speaking, an Episcopal parish choosing a curriculum anew would be better served by calling up the church-owned and sponsored publisher than, say, a fundamentalist Baptist publisher when seeking options.

Is the Episcopal Church "close" enough to Roman Catholicism to share or simply tweak the same curricula for its specific uses? My own opinion is that the person teaching the curriculum makes a huge difference. My own teaching of Catechesis and Godly Play is nearly identical. That is because I am Anglican, and Anglican theology is going to seep into my teaching no matter what program or curriculum I teach.

With that said, there are a couple of important differences between Catechesis and Godly Play which some would find important when choosing one program over the other. The first concerns the Old Testament – Godly Play teaches it; Catechesis does not in programs for younger children. Personally, I love the Old Testament lessons of Godly Play and find them both age appropriate and scripturally sound. My own children love the lessons given in the OT desert box, and I have gained many insights from the OT materials myself. Godly Play is indeed more Trinitarian in its focus and thus more in line with the theology of the Book of Common Prayer than the more Christocentric nature of Catechesis.

Another seemingly small but perhaps important difference is the focus on "wondering" in Godly Play. If the difference between "proclamation" in Catechesis and "wondering" in Godly Play is seen as a notable difference, I might suggest that this difference is not just about words. The Anglican Church does encourage its parishioners to do more "wondering" than the Roman Catholic Church. We Anglicans are encouraged to use our brains to think about theological issues as part our Anglican "three legged stool" of scripture, tradition, and reason. What the Catechists might call Berryman's openness to "the fact that children may go off on their own tangents as they try to make meaning for themselves" might be a reflection of a more Anglican perspective on scripture.

Does all or any of this matter? It depends on your priorities and your goals for Christian formation of children and of adults. What a parish values, what it hopes to accomplish, and what it can realistically pull off will drive the choice between one program or the other. If a parish chooses Godly Play, that might mean the parish chooses to be more in line with Anglican values and the Book of Common Prayer. That might mean the parish is being realistic about what it can offer and what its volunteers can reasonable do. That might mean that adult Christian formation is already in place or that adults will seek their own formation in other, separate ways.

If a parish chooses Godly Play or another Episcopal curriculum for its primary Sunday morning offering, this might simply mean that Catechesis would be better presented in another venue, in another time period, or in some other manner which would allow the Catechists to best use their time, talents, and perhaps consolidate resources on a community wide or other shared basis. The two programs are both great choices for what they are and do not by any means need to be seen as opposing forces.

## Re-Thinking Crafts in Children's Programs

How many times has your child come home from a school, church, or camp program with a "craft" project that has gone straight to the trash? This "craft" likely took little effort or imagination on the part of your child. Your child likely made this "craft" as a means of filling up time, used plastic or other manufactured (and likely imported) materials, and followed a template to make something considered "cute" by the adult leaders. This "craft" may even have been said (by the adult leaders) to somehow enforce a lesson presented. Really?

I would love to re-think the whole meaning and purpose of crafts in children's programs. Why do we have children do "arts & crafts"? What is the purpose of these projects?

Let's start by defining the word "craft." If you look up the word in a dictionary and study the history of crafts, you find that a "craft" – or "handicraft" – is:

- A handmade object that is useful and decorative, and
- Something requiring skill.

So why do we offer crafts in children's programs at all? The making of handicrafts is a part of school curriculums in some countries. The idea is that children will spend time gaining a skill that is useful in real life. This is certainly a worthwhile use of children's time. Learning to knit has been a fulfilling and useful part of my own life, as I've made blankets, sweaters, prayer shawls, and scarves for friends and families to show my love and appreciation of them – along with providing a garment or wrap that they can use. Knitting is a calming pastime and gives me something relatively mindless to do after a long day of work or activity.

Crafts like knitting, carpentry, leatherwork, basket weaving, and the like can give us all something relaxing and fulfilling to do in our spare time. We can express some artistry and create something useful, a personal memento that we've put our time and personality into. Crafts are, in the best sense of the term, a meaningful pastime that can last years or even a lifetime. Crafts are also a means of going off the grid and getting away from the digital world for a time. Crafts are worthy of children's time in our schools and church programs.

But most of the "crafts" offered in children's programs do not live up to the standard of "useful" or "requiring skill." If we're honest, we're simply keeping little fingers busy and out of trouble with many of the "craft" activities we ask children to do. We're simply filling up extra time.

Let me be clear...I'm not dissing true creative responses to lessons or presentations. My favorite part of Jerome Berryman's *Godly Play* program is the opportunity to make a creative response to the scripture presented to children. In my own creative responses to these lessons, I've invariably gained deep insight and understanding of scripture passages and stories. I think all children should have an opportunity to explore lessons freely and artistically. But true creative responses only require very simple art supplies – blank sheets of papers, colored pencils, modelling clay, or other inexpensive and open ended resources. Let's face it: gluing pre-cut pieces of brightly colored foam onto other pre-cut pieces of foam doesn't really tap into anyone's creativity or deepen anyone's understanding of anything.

So here's what I challenge leaders of children's programs to do in their "arts & crafts" activities:

- Think about why you offer an arts & crafts activity – is it to teach a skill, make something useful, or offer a meditative and calming activity during an otherwise busy program?
- Offer a true creative response that tangibly links the activity to your lesson or curriculum – allow children to use their own imaginations and

creativity freely and let them express what the lesson or presentation means to them.

- Be green – use natural, renewable materials instead of materials that eat up fossil fuels and are shipped in from thousands of miles away. Use quality materials that reflect your respect for our Earth.

- Make something that children and their families will actually use and cherish in years to come. Make something worthy of the effort, even if it takes more time and effort to learn and practice a skill and produce something of value.

Let's stop the madness of having children spend precious time making junky items that will go straight to the trash. Let's allow children to actually learn some skills and make something meaningful they can feel good about.

### Re-Thinking the Summer

Long, long ago, in a thriving Methodist church in a small city not far away, I went to Sunday School in the summer. It was unthinkable that I wouldn't. Why in the world would you discontinue an important thing like getting together with folks in your Christian community, just because it's summer?

Why indeed do we Episcopalians discontinue an important means of community-building and faith formation in the summer? Are we all expected to "summer" at our second homes somewhere and forget about our faith? Oh, please.

As a parent, I am always looking for something for my kids to do in the summer. We go from overscheduled, exhausted and sleep-deprived during the school year to under-scheduled, bored, and cabin-fevered in the summer.

For all of us who bemoan children not showing up early on Sunday mornings during the school year, the availability of "only one hour" on Sunday morning to try to teach the essentials of the Bible and our faith, and the ever-challenging task of recruiting volunteers, the summer sure looks like a growth opportunity.

Programs we might want to try out or just use for a change of pace might be offered during a more relaxed summer session. Teenagers too young to work and who would otherwise be sitting around texting might be recruited to help. Adult volunteers willing to help but not willing to commit to an entire year might be willing to sign on for a more limited time of just a couple of months.

The timing of events could also be expanded way beyond the usual one-hour-on-Sunday format. What about a regular weekday morning class, and for a couple of hours? What about an evening class running concurrent with an adult offering or fellowship event? In a recovering economy, what about offering limited or part-time jobs for a few folks (particularly young people) while letting volunteers take a break?

Several directors of Christian education on a national Episcopal listserv have commented that summer is often a time of "church shopping" and moving from place to place by prospective members. Newcomers – those who likely need Christian formation in community the most – might be more inclined to try us out on a trial basis before committing to the regular program year. Summer, then, might be just the time to rev up our Christian formation programs, rather than let them sit on idle.

Cynthia Coe

## Is It Time to Start Paying Formation Teachers?

Every time a child is baptized in the Episcopal Church, the entire congregation vows "to do all in [their] power to support these persons in their life in Christ." What does this mean? If we thought about these words at all, we might expect this means that volunteers would come forth (or be arm-twisted) to teach Sunday School on a regular or irregular basis and pledge money to cover curricula and classroom supplies.

We might forget that catechists may, in the Episcopal Church, be licensed by bishops (and required to receive training). We may even forget that in the early days of Christianity, teaching was a specialty, that teachers were put in the same category as prophets in the *Didache*, to be welcomed, shown hospitality, and supported with food and lodging.

In this 21st century, "all in your power" might mean many new and different methods of formation. If we could suddenly start from scratch and put away all the hand wringing of trying to find quality volunteers willing and able to teach our children in what many of us see as the vital ministry of intentional formation, what would this ministry look like? Would we really resort to asking overscheduled parents to do this for free, even though they may have no experience in education at all, may not really know the basics of the faith themselves, and might not particularly want to teach at all?

I'm not trying to upset the apple cart if you have wonderful volunteers who cheerfully come prepared each Sunday to enthusiastically and skillfully teach your kids. But if you don't, this is perhaps an option to at least consider – it might work for your congregation; it might not. We need new ideas that work, and this may or may not be one of them.

"Where your treasure is, your heart is also." We all say that Christian formation of young people is tremendous important. We all know that times are changing. We all know that the moment in time when women did not "work outside the home" and had time to serve as church volunteers for large chunks of time is over. We want the ministry of formation to be done well, with well trained teachers who know their stuff, come prepared, and are on board with acceptable pedagogical concepts.

So why aren't we willing to pay something for this kind of excellence and dedication? We pay people to answer the phone, take out the trash, make sure the bills get paid, and may even pay them to sing in the choir. But we don't pay people with knowledge, experience, and training to teach our kids basic Bible stories and concepts and explore with them how to apply them to daily life?

This is NOT to say that all parishes should immediately hire numerous teachers for their Christian formation programs (though maybe this would indeed work in your situation). Dioceses could offer quality formation classes in the summer, perhaps at diocesan camps. Several small congregations could go in together and hold quarterly retreats or other quality offerings. Episcopal schools could offer weekend or weekday afterschool programs to children who do not attend the day school for academic classes.

The point is, there are many, many ways the Episcopal Church could offer formation programs in more effective ways than relying solely on volunteers with little or no preparation or training. And with a shaky economy, couldn't we find some folks who would gladly take on this task for a small honorarium or part time salary?

Ten years ago, my parish did indeed offer two-hour Tuesday morning classes for preschoolers, along with Wednesday afternoon classes from 4:00 to 6:00. The classes were full, and parents paid a small materials fee and made sure children were there every week. A couple of the teachers were paid church staff members. The rest of the teachers had undergone hundreds of hours of training and should have been paid. In any case, we had a terrific program that was well attended and much appreciated by parents. Now, the moms of children in our parish have full or part time jobs practicing law or working as sales reps. They have not – and likely wouldn't – go through hours upon hours of training that moms were willing to undertake just ten years ago. Times have changed, and our methods of formation may well need to change with them. In any case, we need to keep our eye on the ball – what indeed is the most effective way we can offer formation programs in this new 21st century?

## Advocating Children's Gifts & Talents

One of the most transformational learning experiences I've ever had was a six-week "Gifts & Talents" course at my local parish. Both the content and the methodology of the course was the Church at its best – the class was affirmative, practical, helped me truly find my calling, and helped me make some wonderful and close friends.

The theory of the course is simple – all of us are individuals. All of us have specific and perhaps even unique callings. We all need to follow our passions. We need to do what we enjoy and what we are good at. We should feel free to say "no" to volunteer recruitment requests that are "not our thing." The most amazing part of all – usually when you draw up a list of tasks needed for a big project, someone will have the gifts needed for individual tasks, and you will likely have all your bases covered to get the project done.

The only big hang-up I had with this course was that it was set solely in the context of the Church. After several excellent self-inventories, you and your small group would name your gifts and seek to plug you into several ministries within the church community. For those of us who have ended up working professionally in the Church, this was great. But I always wondered, what if your true "ministry" was outside the church walls?

That question has continued to nag me, especially as I see plenty of people doing terrific and fulfilling work as volunteers or professionals working for a multitude of non-profits, private businesses, in schools, or out in the community. And if we are serious about "seeking and serving" others in Christ, wherever they may be, shouldn't we honor those "ministries" just as much as "ministries" within the church?

I wonder if the Church - in its role as a prophetic voice - might make a valuable contribution to our culture by holding up the idea that we all have individual gifts and talents that should be pursued. In our society, we have a multitude of needs and a multitude of roles for those in (and out) of our work force to play. We need doctors; but we also need folks to conscientiously and with kindness clean up elderly people in our nursing homes, too. We people to drive trucks, construct buildings, and put cars and other machines together, as much as we need scientists, computer programmers, and physicists.

As we push our children towards so called "higher" standards, I worry that we are not keeping the simple theory of Gifts & Talents in mind. Not everybody should go to college. Not everybody should go to various vocational schools, either. As a society, wouldn't it serve us all best if we spent more time discerning each child's gifts and talents, then tailored educational opportunities accordingly? As we seek to serve our own children in guiding them towards the people they are called to be, I would hope that we would truly see each child as a unique individual, with specific learning styles, learning objectives, and each with a place in this world where his or her talents can be utilized. I would hope that in all our workplaces and ministries, we would appreciate that it's all about gifts & talents, all about finding our true callings.

## Teaching About Hunger

Hunger is a key mission focus of the Church. Yet how do we "teach" about it?

The challenge of providing easy-to-do lesson plans hits a wall against the complexity of why various people might be hungry. The reasons people face hunger are wildly diverse and often complex. These issues don't lend themselves well to quick activities or one hour mission projects.

People in the United States might visit an emergency food pantry because they are short on cash after paying the monthly bills. Others may visit the very same food pantry on regular basis because of long term unemployment, disability, high health care tabs, or unexpected costs resulting from disasters personal or community-wide.

In other countries, hunger might result from lack of clean water, deforestation, drought, crop failures, war, lack of infrastructure to sell crops or to finance farming related businesses, unfair trade practices, or many, many other factors. So to "teach" about hunger, you will likely need to introduce the ins and outs of farming, fair trade, scarcity of resources, social justice, and the disparity of standards of living across the globe.

## Sustainability is Key

The alleviation of hunger is not, in many cases, about simply handing out food. A huge focus of church mission work is about sustainability – working with people to ensure that they will both have food and continue to have food on an on-going basis. This task is not simple in the least and requires much work. Those who are themselves in need must be involved in the process, or the problem will not be solved. However, when sustainable solutions are found, the chances of successfully keeping people fed are much higher in the long run than simple hand-outs.

## Self-Respect is a Christian Virtue

Then there's the issue of respecting those in need. Part of the Episcopal Church's Baptismal Covenant is to respect the dignity of every single person. That's part of who we are as a Church. This means we don't want to keep people in the role of victims. We don't want them permanently dependent on hand-outs if they are capable of fending for themselves eventually. We seek to aid and build up communities, not keep them forever as our own personal charity cases. It's about them; it's not about us.

Christian Nurture in the Twenty-First Century

<u>We Might be Challenged Ourselves</u>

In addressing the issues of hunger, we might find ourselves uncomfortably challenged to examine our own habits, extravagances, and demands. In current American culture, we want the best quality goods and foods –and lots of them – but we also want to pay the lowest price possible. Do we care that our demands for low prices means someone else gets paid a very low wage and might not be able to adequately feed their family? Do we care about the working conditions of those who produced that $5 shirt we just snapped up at the big-box store as the terrific bargain?

And why don't we do more to help those in desperate need around the world? Is it because we're buying more and more clothes to pack our already full closets? Remodeling the kitchen or bath to make sure our houses aren't "dated"? What about our faith communities – how much do we spend on the core mission of feeding the hungry, compared with how much we might spend on other items in the budget? Not pleasant questions to tackle, are they?

Challenging though these questions might be, feeding the hungry and providing clean water to the thirsty are core missions of the Church. Addressing these questions might cause us to dramatically simplify our lifestyles, pay more for products we enjoy, and even open our eyes to a world of social injustices large and small.

Yet this is what Christianity is all about: turning our lives and the world upside down, just to make sure everybody might enjoy a simple, nutritious meal.

Tips for Teaching About Hunger

- Alleviating hunger is not cute, trite, or "fun." Please, please, please let your lesson plans reflect this.
- Please don't use food as craft materials or game tokens. The food you waste in doing so could feed a lot of people. Food is precious to many in our world.
- Teaching children about hunger by depriving them of food is not a good idea. Many children may have issues of malnutrition themselves. Better to serve healthy food and point out the gift that this food can be.
- Do teach about hunger! This is a core focus of Christianity, as is "seeking and serving Christ in others."
- Hunger is generally not a topic that can be addressed in a quick and easy lesson. Plan on an on-going discussion of this topic.

# Youth Ministry in the Real World

## Essays on Youth Ministry in the Twenty-First Century

## Youth Ministry – Remembering Who We Are

I once consulted with a parish that, seemingly, was doing everything "right" in their youth ministry. After their youth ministry had crashed following the departure of a full time and beloved youth minister several years ago, the parish very much wanted to reach out to the teenagers in their community. In the past year, they have recruited mature, dedicated teachers who are well prepared and enthusiastic. They adopted a curriculum designed by an Episcopal seminary that has been very well received. They have excellent facilities, a new staff person, and a budget to support all these efforts.

Yet…very few youth attend these wonderful programs. I was asked, "what more can we do, when we seem to be doing all we possibly *can* do?" I was forced to say, "I don't know." I was forced to tell them that "the church" generally is facing a whole new world in youth ministry and hasn't quite figured out what to do about youth ministry. Clearly, the tried and true methods of youth ministry from the recent past are not working.

Our lunch discussion among parents of teens pointed to many challenges in reaching out to teens. Homework has increased astronomically in the last few years, particularly for teens hoping to attend college.

Teens are chronically sleep deprived, due to increased academic expectations. If teens are involved in extra-curricular activities (sports, scouts, service organizations, theatre programs, band, you-name-it, and yes, church youth groups, too), these organizations also have their own time and attention requirements that add to the collective stress of teens and their parents alike.

Sports are no longer just something fun to do. In the car this morning, my daughter told me of a friend who has a metal plate in his shoulder due to sports injuries and deals with chronic pain at age 16. My own daughter busted both ankles and retired from gymnastics at age 14, and her boyfriend ended his football career at age 15 due to injuries.

And then there are the deaths. In one issue of the Knoxville News-Sentinel, the obituaries included the deaths of 3 teens – two aged 14 and one 17 year old who died in a car wreck which also critically injured her 16 year old sister. (I've had to post condolences to one of my teen Facebook friends over that one.) Those with whom I consulted this weekend also had similar tragedies in their own community.

So what's a church to do? Here are three thoughts:

Reaching Out: A small glimpse of where youth

ministry might go came to me when, as this parish listed the "positives" of their program, one woman raised her hand and said, "my daughter doesn't attend church, but I really appreciate that the church still sends her birthday cards and hasn't forgotten her." I could relate. My son no longer attends church, but both he and I were touched that the acolyte leader emailed me recently and asked about my son, showing that he had not been forgotten, either. Remembering is important; remembering is a large part of who we are.

Remembering Who We Are: Several friends who attend a Methodist church here in Knoxville told me that several years ago, their congregation decided to stop doing "country club type activities," because this "wasn't what their church was about." They instead focused on building Habitat for Humanity houses, a food pantry for the hungry, and an addiction recovery ministry. As a result of cutting the "country club stuff" and focusing, instead, on "what we are really about," the congregation went from a membership of 700 to 4,000 (and no, that's not a typo – four *thousand* members, and an Average Sunday Attendance of 3,000).

What are we "really about?" And what is ministry to youth "really about?" Are we involving teens in what our churches are "really about?" Many schools now require teens to serve in their communities as part of their high school graduation requirements. To my surprise, my own teens eagerly serve as Salvation Army bell ringers, fundraiser party hosts, and elementary school tutors. Are our churches actively participating in these efforts to empower youth to serve their communities?

<u>Reclaiming A Prophetic Voice</u>: Teens are sorely in need of Sabbath. Teens are sorely in need of pastoral care. These are areas in which the church historically excels. Yet we may find ourselves addressing the huge number of teens who do not choose or find time to attend church by simply complaining that they don't make our programs a priority – focusing perhaps on our needs to be affirmed in our efforts, rather the teens' needs themselves.

Instead of simply complaining about the few number of teens who attend our churches, might we serve these youth better by speaking out about the issues facing them? What does the church have to say about the concepts of Sabbath, rest, and not trying to be all things to all people? What would we say to teens (or anyone) overextending themselves to the point of injury? Are we sharing these messages out in the world?

Jesus did not expect people to come to him; he went out to where they were. We may need to think about reaching outward ourselves, instead of simply hoping to pull teens in.

# Christian Nurture in the Twenty-First Century

## Confessions of a Gym Mom

## ...or why my children (and I) didn't go

## to church youth group

*"He brought me out into an open place;"* Psalm18:20a

I did not take my children to youth group. There. I've confessed.

Do I feel bad about this? Well....no. And where were we? The gym - spending hours upon hours while my daughter trained as a competitive gymnast under the tutelage of former coaches of the Soviet Olympic team. And did my whole family experience community, transformation, and a lived faith during this time? Well....yes, we did.

During the long hours of waiting for my daughter to finish up practice on "Russian time" (the practice ends when the Russian coach says it ends, which could be any time), I got to know people from near and far, whom I might never have met otherwise. I met recent immigrants from Europe, children of Iraqi immigrants, children adopted from Ukraine, adults who had endured life under Communism, as well as Tennesseans and other

Americans from all walks of life.

We all agonized over our children's training and hoped they wouldn't break any bones or seriously pull a muscle. We had meals together and get-togethers. We got to know each other's families. Siblings were, by necessity, taken along to weekend meets out of town, and I visited parts of the country I would never have thought to visit on my own. Our family spent time together while on the road.

My daughter learned resilience – something that is a huge part of our faith, but that we might not do such a great job of teaching within the church. My proudest moment as a mother was seeing her fall off the balance beam during the state championships, then get right back on the beam and finish her routine. Life requires this skill; we all fall off our balance beams at some point and need to just plain get back on it.

I learned some things, too. Watching coaches at the top of their game taught me volumes about the art of teaching that informs my work every day. I also learned how much my own country had changed since my childhood, when every single person at a lunch table moaned and commiserated about their personal struggles with the INS office in Nashville – all of us had reason to have visited this place to sort out immigration applications.

At some point, of course, it did occur to me that it was a little strange that extremely qualified international coaches had settled in Knoxville, Tennessee. I learned about the crash of the Russian economy in 1998 – a fact that had not penetrated my little world. I happened upon an ad seeking parents for cute little babies, and learned that there are 143 million orphans in the world – a fact that also had somehow eluded me.

One thing led to another, and my family ended up on the Arctic Coast of Russia, adding to our family with one such cute little baby. We were assisted by a coach who put through calls to us from family back home, speaking Russian to the hotel switchboard operator and, when we arrived back home, helped to calm our new baby by speaking his native language. My friends learned that children they had grown up thinking of as "not children you would want" were actually good looking, smart, athletic, and a joy to have around.

And, after total burnout as a parish DCE – ministering to others after seemingly everyone in America went into melt-down after 9/11, a rash of suicides in my parish, and split of the parish into three in 2003 – I found my faith again. God definitely has a sense of humor - my own dark night of the soul had its culmination in the near total darkness of an Arctic winter, with blizzard conditions and zero visibility. When I returned, I had a new mission and new faith. Eventually, I even got back to work in the church again.

Faith is out in the world. Faith is practiced wherever we are. Faith is making friends with people we might have nothing in common with but who love us and we them for these very differences. Faith is ministering to the people right smack in front of us, wherever that might be. Faith is going where we might be called, even (and especially) if it's not in the church building itself.

## Feeding Twinkies

"Childhood obesity rates continue to rise," ran the crawler on the cable news channel this afternoon. While this excess refers to food eaten by many children in America, this "rate of obesity" could also refer to the amount of material goods we give children, the amount of activities we cram into their schedules, and even the quality of their spiritual formation.

This excess is, unfortunately, the downside to a very affluent, very blessed American culture. During my travels in Russia a few years ago, I lost weight without trying. With no McDonald's, Starbucks, or Tex-Mex anywhere in sight, I ate only what I actually needed. I ate the simple but protein-rich food offered at our hotel's buffet every morning as my main meal, then had only hot tea for lunch and a little bit of bread and cheese for dinner. It was plenty.

My time in Russia was equally stripped down and wonderfully bare boned. With the quiet of the Arctic winter essentially confining us to hotel and baby home visits, I had time to read, knit, and spend hours playing with my new son and doing nothing else, with no distractions. Life back in America is usually far more complicated.

Looking at church programs and curricula that

scream, "fun!" "exciting!" and "NEW," I'm reminded of similar marketing used to push excessive restaurant meals and entertainment to our children. Do we really need these luxuries (and compared to the way most people on this earth live, yes, they are luxuries)? What's wrong with *quiet*, *simple*, and even *ancient*? Are my children being fed the spiritual equivalent of twinkies?

The food of our faith is simple bread and wine – that's all. We don't need twinkies in our spiritual lives. What we and our children need is simple: real and authentic faith, a chance to learn the stories and the concepts of the Christian journey, and a chance to think and talk and practice what these stories and concepts mean in our own lives and in the world. More and more excess is the last thing any of us need.

There is nothing wrong with fun in and of itself. Joy and pleasure would, I hope, be part of all of our Christian journeys. Jesus himself attended his share of weddings, feasts, dinners, and other "fun" social occasions.

But "fun" is not our whole story, just as dessert is not the whole meal. The main course of our story is loving God with all our hearts, minds, and souls and loving our neighbors as ourselves. Fun and fellowship are the chocolate cake.

If "fun" is all we offer, we are not being true to ourselves, and we might even be guilty of false advertising. And if "fun" is all we offer, we might be serving those who come to us for spiritual nurture and guidance nothing more than a plate of twinkies.

Christian Nurture in the Twenty-First Century

## Youth Ministry @ Home

My teens no longer attend youth group. My teens no longer attend church. Say what you will. Go ahead and flame me. But it's not like I can hold a gun to their heads and "make them go," as many would have me do.

In reading the book, *You Lost Me: Why Young Christians Are Leaving Church…and Rethinking Faith* by David Kinnaman, I found much which resonated with my own faith journey. My big hang-up with this book? The views of those who feel the institutional church is out of touch with contemporary society seems more in line with those my age than just "young adults." We are, in fact, seeing a second generation of "young adults" who say to the institutional church, "you lost me."

Does this mean my teens are not engaged in an active youth ministry, supported by their parents? Far from it. We do "youth ministry" on practically a daily basis. And it's important work that I can feel really good about.

My views on Christian formation are right in line with that genius of 19$^{th}$ century Christian education, Horace Bushnell – author of the excellent book *Christian Nurture*. Bushnell taught that Christian formation is best done at home, by the children's own parents. The Christian education of his own family consisted by picnics after church on Sunday afternoons, selecting a question written on a slip of paper by a family member of something they wanted to discuss, and attempting to answer those questions, one by one.

As many of us wring our hands, trying to figure out what to "do" about the situation, I suggest that maybe Horace Bushnell had the right idea. I must say that I really and truly don't blame my kids for not wanting to drive through rush-hour traffic on I-40 on a school night to sit in a church basement or go play laser tag, when they have a gazillion homework assignments they must do…or flunk high school.

Teens need something more basic, something more meaningful, something that meets them where they are. My own teens frequently bring home friends – romantically involved or otherwise – to dinner. I'm finding that almost all of these young people come from families in distress. Their parents might be in the midst of a divorce. They might be losing their homes to foreclosure. Their families are likely struggling financially. All of them are severely pressured to make good grades in difficult courses and get into colleges that are increasingly difficult to get into.

So the "youth ministry" my husband and I find ourselves doing – almost on a weekly basis – is simply putting a hot meal on the table and inviting these young people to sit down and participate in "normal" two-parent family life, warts and all. The kitchen is usually half-chaotic, the family room usually needs a clean-up, and the seven year old sometimes finds himself in a time-out for ungentlemanly behavior right in the middle of dinner. The dog is always underfoot, and Dad's experiments in cooking are usually successfully, but sometimes not. The silverware doesn't match.

But we try. Everyone is asked to give a report on their day, and we probably shouldn't be surprised that each and every teen who comes through this daily ritual does indeed give us a "report" on what they've been doing and doesn't seem to mind at all the barely-controlled chaos of our household. No one yet has balked at our practice of holding hands around the dinner table and praying before the meal.

As St. Francis once said, "preach…and if you have to, use words." In this new era of post-Christianity, we are looking not only at "young adults" who say, "you lost me," but also the children of middle aged parents who are exiled from the church and hurting. In this continuing spiral of those who feel this exile, perhaps a return to the basics of a decent meal, fellowship, and walking the walk by ordinary laypeople might go much further than any "program" any of us might invent.

### Stop the Madness

Simplify. Americans are being hit with this term more and more, especially in these economic challenging times. As I turned on the news this morning, I encountered a story about a young man who had given away most of what he owned – and was perfectly happy doing so. Then, I turned on my laptop to see a featured story on "The Secrets of Billionaires." Duh - you take public transportation, wear jeans and a t-shirt, and don't waste your money on a lot of "luxury" crap you don't need.

I wonder if this can be applied to issues of time and effort, too. I'm reminded of Alec Baldwin's character on 30 Rock, exhorting his staff to "go down to go up." After his career hits a wall, he takes a job in the mail room, only to work himself back up the ladder and back on top again.

These concepts do have scriptural basis – give all your possessions away if you really want to follow Christ, take a seat at the end of the table and wait to be asked to move up. These concepts presented by the 21st century media are certainly not new. They are firmly part of the Christian tradition, but ones we might not be so good at putting into practice in our own lives.

Could this concept of stripping ourselves down to the bare essentials apply to our ministries in this 21$^{st}$ century as well? Do we need to strip down to the bare essentials, focus on the basics, and grow from there?

In my own household, my husband and I have struggled recently the challenges of parenting two teenagers. We've been reading *Hurt: Inside the World of Today's Teenagers*," by Chap Clark. We read that our children likely feel abandoned by us, by their churches, by just about everyone. As we discerned how to deal with issues facing us, a clergy friend invited one of our children to participate in a youth group that specialized in helping teens struggling with all sorts of issues. It seemed to be just the thing. "But wait," my husband pointed out, "aren't we abandoning our child once again by sending our child to yet another program?" So we have just plain spent more time with our child, and the problems have ceased – as simple as that. We didn't need a "program," as high quality and well intentioned as I'm sure it was.

As much time as I've spent organizing programs, I'm wondering if "one more program" is really what we all need. At the same time, I see the need to teach the "basics" of the faith and for parents to simply spend more time with their own children. If we take our children to "one more program," even in church, that is time we as parents are *not* spending with them.

I'm not saying, "ditch Sunday School." Really, I'm not. What I am saying is that our children are seriously overscheduled, as are most of us. I'm saying something has got to give, and we as Christians may need to take the lead in saying, "enough." We may need to walk the walk, even as we talk the talk.

## Keepin' it Real

I found myself doing youth ministry today - totally off the cuff, totally unexpectedly, and after one of those moments when you feel like you have a spotlight shining on you that says, "you – now – drop what you're doing and do this now."

It began as a pause in a busy day at the Kroger Starbucks with my 15 year old daughter, her friend, and my 6 year old son. We had just a couple of minutes before heading off to the Wednesday noon service, and I had agreed to bring lunch. When the question of whether the girls would attend the service or simply "hang out" and babysit the little brother while I attended alone, my daughter's friend surprised me by saying yes, she might like to go.

"I go to church, but I don't like it. They are always asking us for money. I want to find a church where they are keepin' it real." Gulp. I had to sheepishly tell her that this is what I wanted too, that honestly, there had been quite a number of pleas for money at the regular Sunday service lately, though they were all for good causes.

This honesty on my part opened a floodgate for this young girl to open up and tell me all about her broken family, their struggles, how they were recovering from a lot of bad stuff. We talked all the way up Kingston Pike on the drive to church about some fairly deep subjects. I was impressed that despite troubling times, this young woman had a great relationship with her mother – one that most moms of teenagers would hope to have with their kids.

As a first time visitor to my church, this young woman did not hesitate to ask hard questions of us. As soon we as entered the church building, she pulled me aside to say, "you're supposed to tithe 10% of your money and give it to the church. I want to know, where does the money go to?" A great question, and one that each of us should ask and hold the church accountable for!

Did we manage to "keep it real"? I hope so. My daughter's friend was immediately impressed with the gentle, welcoming smile of our female priest. I was glad my daughter's friend was able to attend a service where we didn't pass the plate, where we spend as much time as needed to allow each and every person to receive individual prayers and laying on of hands at the altar rail, where everybody passes the peace with everybody else in the service. My six year old participated by humming with the hymns all during the healing prayers.

So contrary to my assumption that these two teenage girls would be bored to tears by a small, quiet, no-frills service with lunch around a workroom table, I was blessed to see the girls eagerly pitching in to help set out food, meet the others attending the service, and participating in the liturgy. Despite no children's chapel and nothing seemingly "kid friendly" about this day, my six year old told me he liked the service very much, especially the lunch – the community. For me, that's as real as it gets.

## The Importance of Being Empowered

While leading a Sunday morning youth class, using a curriculum I designed and wrote, I found myself facing a group of middle school boys, none of whom looked particularly eager to be in my class. I knew I would have to do something quickly, or I would lose what little of their attention I had.

I asked, "Who has a good reading voice?" A couple of them mumbled that they did. I handed them the opening prayer and litany for the class and asked them to lead it. They asked who should do what; I told them they looked like smart fellows and to figure it out. Surprisingly, the boys who claimed not to have good reading voices emerged as the readers of the litany – of their own free will. The guys were suddenly engaged in the class, and we had a wonderful and lively discussion of the concepts at hand.

Did these pre-teens do a perfect job of leading worship? No, but that was not at all the point. I knew what the litany said; I didn't need to hear it perfectly. The point was that these young men took charge, led the class, and became in engaged in the important topics of clean water, extreme poverty, and what they might do about these issues.

And isn't this the whole point of Christian formation – letting others step up to the plate, take the lead, and perhaps even take over a ministry? We say one of our primary tasks in our church is to respect the dignity of each and every human being. We say we want to seek and serve Christ in others. So doesn't that mean maybe we should also help each and every young person get to the point of taking on ministries for themselves, to empower them to do ministry on their own?

Christian formation is lifelong, so perhaps we might even think about continuing to empower adults in each of their ministries as well. Do we really believe what we say when we talk about each person having dignity and being valuable as part of the Body of Christ? Do we really believe each and every person has a ministry and a contribution to make?

If this is so, then doesn't that mean we should really, really work on empowering the folks in our pews to truly take on ministries and then step back and let them do what they are called to do? It's a little scary to think about, isn't it? We might have to give some things up; others might not do things the way we think they should be done. We might even find that we need to move on and do something other than what we are doing now.

But we might also find ourselves liberated and fulfilled. I sure had an easy time teaching class last Sunday. I handed the opening prayer and litany to a teenage girl who had that "I hate this place and really don't want to be here" look on her face; she instantly perked up and became engaged in the class. A middle school teacher with experience in organic farming read the meditation and started a good discussion among the kids (even though the lesson plan called for silence – no matter; it worked). A member of the vestry read the printed lesson. She then began a discussion of how even small donations to others in need could make a huge difference in their lives.

I was left to sit back and take it all in. I couldn't have done better myself.

Christian Nurture in the Twenty-First Century

## Are We On a Mission...or Just a Trip?

### Know Before You Go

Watching an interview with Rep. John Lewis (D – Ga.) on a television news show, I was struck by how much time and focus he and his colleagues in the Civil Rights Movement put into the sheer study of the philosophy and discipline of non-violent protest. Before embarking on their first sit-in or freedom march, Lewis and students from Vanderbilt, Meharry Medical School, Fisk University, and Tennessee State University met every Tuesday evening in Nashville to study and ponder and do disciplined academic work together. Clearly, their work in preparing for their mission of transformation of our society paid off, serving as a model many of us might follow.

As we embark on our own missions, I wonder if we do our homework before we go off to minister to others, both here and abroad? In his book ***Toxic Charity***, Robert D. Lupton unequivocally says, "no." He says we fail to consider how best to serve those we hope to serve on mission trips. He tells us we often would be better off hiring local people to do the hands-on work we regularly send our youth off to do in the summer. Worse yet, he says we are turning the poor in developing nations into beggars, dependent on our continued donations rather than developing their own economies. We might even be contributing to the erosion of the dignity of those we seek to serve.

Do our "missionaries" - decked out in matching t-shirts, luggage bulging with hand-outs at our local airport check-ins - know this? Maybe they have stopped to think about it, maybe not. My own brother emailed me from the coast of Africa recently, asking if there wasn't a better way for the Navy to aid people in ports they visited, other than simply handing out inexpensive school supplies. This was a great teachable moment to tell him what my own church was doing and how we were doing things differently.

Lupton's book challenges us to have many teachable moments – and hopefully teachable hours, days, and weeks – before we book that trip to Central America, Africa, or other places we think might simply need suitcases full of medical supplies, a paint job for the local orphanage, and our smiling presence. We need to ask hard questions.

We also need to think about long term consequences and plans. We need to find out what is really needed and who best to do that – even if it might not be us. As Lupton rather graphically points out, the cost of one student mission trip to Central America to paint an orphanage could, instead, have funded the cost of hiring two local painters, two full time teachers, and new uniforms for every child in the local school. Know these realities before you go.

Yet this is not to say that all travel to other countries is bad. My own travels abroad have made me who I am, changed and opened my mind to many alternate ways of life, and made me re-examine how my own country functions. Hearing stories of those who have been on mission trips to other countries, I have been impressed with how these trips have truly changed the lives and outlooks of those who have gone on these trips.

Knowing about other cultures is a good thing. Exposing our youth to other cultures is a very good thing. Finding out what is really going on in other parts of the world is essential. We want young people to know how the other 99% of people on this earth live. We want them to view other people with respect and appreciation. We want them to truly seek and serve others in Christ – but from a standpoint of understanding, openness to new knowledge, thoughtfulness, and even humility.

So where does this leave our "youth mission trips"? As we embark on a re-figuring of our ministries of formation and mission, do these trips still have a place? I would suggest that yes, they do, but perhaps with different goals and objectives. The spiritual discipline of making a pilgrimage is practically as old as

Christianity itself. Going away and getting out of one's bubble is a time-honored means of spiritual formation.

Likewise, service projects should not be the baby thrown out with the bath water. Hands-on service projects are still needed in certain circumstances: when really needed, where our youth are truly invited to participate, and when those they serve are empowered and treated with dignity for their actual needs.

Mission trips might simply be called "pilgrimages." We might send those who would likely influence others in their communities on "study trips" and specifically ask them to speak, write, blog and Facebook post what they observe.

Going elsewhere is good, but we likely need to think about who is going and why and ask our travelers to put a significant amount of time into preparation and study – along with spreading the message of new knowledge when they return.

Service trips might well be carried out in our own hometowns and neighborhoods, working alongside our neighbors to accomplish mutual goals, such as putting in community gardens or doing neighborhood clean-ups, rather than assuming that "those in need" are someone someplace else.

Service can be carried out within our own

families, in our own homes, and certainly down the block and a few miles away. We absolutely do not need to go halfway around the globe to be of service.

Above all, we might all seek to be smarter about our missions. Study. Think about what we're doing. Prepare on a scale proportional to the mission itself. And know what it is and whom we really serve before we go.

## What is the Purpose of Confirmation Preparation?

### (And Will Tech Do the Job?)

A conversation amongst Episcopal Christian educators took place about one diocese's plan to design an "online" confirmation class. Many CED professionals have chimed in with numerous high tech ideas, including use of power point slides, online blackboards, chat rooms, and the like.

For maybe the first time in my life, I find myself chiming in with…"maybe online isn't the way to go; maybe the old fashioned in-person method is best." Did the person who loves tapping on her laptop more than anything, smartphone by her side, really say THAT?!

Yep. Confirmation is the process of becoming an adult member of the church, whether that person is a new adult coming into the Episcopal Church or a teenager coming of age and "owning" the Baptismal Vows taken for her or him as a small child. It's about discipleship. It's about becoming a minister in your own right. It's about stepping up to the plate and becoming an active member of the community.

This community aspect of confirmation is where the high tech gadgets and resources lose me.

## Christian Nurture in the Twenty-First Century

Resources are dearly needed – that is without a doubt. And as far as conveying pure information about the church, online via the web is the way to go. Resources available online are generally free, readily available to most adults, can be revised or improved in a matter of minutes, disseminated within seconds and can be read and digested on the participant's own time frame with the click of a few keys.

But...in my mind, the whole purpose of confirmation preparation is welcoming new people and teens into the community and guiding them into discipleship. It's not just about the information. So many times, I think confirmation classes tend to simply "tell" folks about the history of the church and parish, give them talks about the ministries the parish might do, and maybe impart some knowledge about the liturgy and theology of the Episcopal Church.

What I fear most parishes are not doing are practicing prayer with people, taking them personally through a process of finding themselves as ministers in their own parish, and working with them and alongside them in going through a process of true Christian formation and transformation.

So here's what I would love to see: high quality, free confirmation resources available to any parish that will use them. These would be used in combination with local parish groups made up of mature Christians, current parish members, and newcomers. Prospective confirmands would get to know each other AND current members. Community would be formed, the group would grow together and everyone would learn something from everyone else. A gifts & talent component would be help newcomers identify the best ways they might become ministers themselves.

Would this be a new and different way of doing things? Yes. Would it take effort and willingness to change? Yes. Would it pay off in more committed new members, renewal of current members, and better use of church resources? I think so. The times, they are a changing. More and more young adults describe themselves as "spiritual not religious." We need to do something different.

**Adult Spiritual Growth and Discipleship:
Essays on Lifelong Christian Formation**

## What Would "Missionary Society" Formation Look Like?

The Episcopal Church has sought to re-brand itself as the "Missionary Society." Generally, I like this re-branding. Most real life is experienced out in the world, not within the walls of a church building for a couple of hours a week.

In keeping with this re-branding, should we also re-think our Christian formation programs? If we focus our efforts on equipping our members for "mission" out in the world, do we need to radically re-focus our efforts to "form" people to function as missionaries in their everyday lives and as they live and work outside the Church?

Here are some ideas of what we might seek to accomplish as central objectives of Missionary Society formation:

- Create awareness of the needs and issues around us: Inside a lovely church building or living in suburban America, we may honestly not know what is going on in our cities, in our regions, or in other parts of the world. Before we seek to send others out into the mission field, we might highlight needs and urge parishioners to actively read up or think about needs around them.

- Equip missioners with the basics of the Christian faith: We need to offer "basics" courses on scripture, theology, and how we might address needs as Christians. Often, we ask for volunteers to "help" with various ministries without any reflection or theological basis for doing the work in the first place.

- Skills building: If we want missions to be successful and effective, we might offer training in subjects like pastoral care, language skills, fundraising, asset-based community development, causes of poverty, and other helpful tools. Training could be offered by networks or on a regional or diocesan basis.

- Support and Companionship: Fellowship with others working in a mission field is often one of the most rewarding parts of any ministry. Intentional efforts to offer support groups for those in similar ministries might go a long way towards preventing burn-out and supporting on-going efforts.

- On-going Praxis: What do we learn from ministry? What often do we stop to think about incidents in our ministries and how they form and inform our faith? Regular times and places to do just this might be terrific means of actually "doing" lifelong formation.

These programs could be offered via online courses, in person, in small groups, diocesan-wide, or through regional weekend retreats. Some of these topics are offered in seminary to M. Div students or for clergy as continuing education. But if we want to function truly as a Missionary Society, we need to make this support and these tools available to all laity – a radical but likely necessary step as we continue to re-think the Church.

## We're Stuck – Spiritual Growth, A Lifelong Process

"I already know everything I need to know," responded a man by-passing an invitation to my Christian Ed class one Sunday at a Knoxville area church. And how many of us working in the church, especially in CED, have heard that from our parishioners? How many of us have also heard, "religion is out, spirituality is in"?

Two books connect these dots, taking us on journeys through adult spiritual growth and development. In *Mansions of the Heart: Exploring the Seven Stages of Spiritual Growth*, Thomas Ashbrook leads us through a contemporary, plain-language pilgrimage through Teresa of Avila's *Interior Castle*, her analogy for the stages of spiritual growth, written in the 16th century. On the far less mystical side, *Christian Formation: Integrating Theology and Human Development* (ed. James R. Estep and Jonathan H. Kim) makes the strong case for lifelong spiritual development, how it happens and how it could be facilitated by the institutional church. Both of these books start from very, very different perspectives but end up at about the same place: we're stuck.

In *Mansions of the Heart*, Ashbrook quotes a startling and brutally honest survey result: there is no correlation between participation in the ministries of the church surveyed and personal spiritual growth. Ouch.

## Christian Nurture in the Twenty-First Century

The problem: lack of clear reference points or processes to aid adults' progress in their spiritual maturity. (In other words, the ministry of Christian formation for adults is not getting the job done.) He advocates better leadership, more resources, and an environment that nurtures what God wants to do in each person's life. As it is, Ashbrook asserts, most people who attend churches are stuck in Teresa's "third mansion" - regular church attendance and participation, but a prayer life that is more talking to God than listening. We then become stuck in this stage, becoming ever more disillusioned or bored or fed up with the institutional church as something deep within us yet yearns for spiritual growth.

From a more developmental perspective, the collection of articles in *Christian Formation* point to the same conclusion and recommend very similar guide posts: varied age related materials and resources, developmentally sound resources (e.g. small group, experiential learning, recognizing the experience adult learners bring to the table – as opposed to talking head "instruction"). Though said quite differently, these articles clearly correspond with ancient mystics: adult spiritual formation is lifelong and ever-changing and growing in response to God and to our own changing circumstances and efforts.

Interestingly, both books also point us to an

issue perhaps few of us want to tackle – the issue of personal responsibility for our own spiritual growth. While we may look to "the church" to cater to us – even present a menu of nutritious courses for growth in front of us – it's ultimately up to us to grow, or not. We can be hit by the bolt of lightning, experience something profound, but what, ultimately, do we do with it? And could that not be said of the Body of Christ itself?

## Changing Adult Hearts and Minds

How do we "learn"? How do we become transformed? What changes our minds on matters large and small?

Discussions on how best to engage adults have cropped up recently on several platforms. Do we provide a "sage on a stage" to get our points across? Do we ask adults what they want and give it to them? Or something else?

It depends, I think, on what you intend to accomplish. What exactly IS the point of adult Christian formation? (And once we tackle that question, we might be in a better position to figure how best to "do" adult formation.)

I would start the conversation by suggesting that there are basically three goals of adult formation:

- Providing basic information about our faith, who we are, what we do, and how we do it
- Transforming people in the imitation of Christ
- Providing skills and tools to do ministry of all kinds

In providing basic information about the faith (and maybe in certain kinds of skill training), the "sage on the stage" method might be a decent way of accomplishing this objective. We would hope that these sages would take advantage of what most of us know as effective teaching strategies – using visual aids, appealing to auditory and kinesthetic learners, keeping presentations crisp, interesting, and relevant.

But what about the objective of transforming adults of all ages and stages towards what we say is the goal of our faith, becoming more Christ-like? How exactly do we do that?

Like any large task, we likely need to use a strong combination of strategies and approaches. The old lecture method might get the ball rolling on transformation, but if that is all we offer people in the way of true transformation, they will quickly find themselves in a rut (and become disillusioned, bored, leave, etc.). We likely will need to tap a number of disciplines, and fortunately, we as a society have a wealth of knowledge and collective experience to use in this task of transformation, to wit:

- Andragogy (adult education, as opposed to pedagogy – children's educational theory). There's a number of texts on how adults learn, particularly in the HR world. We might want to think about Malcolm Knowles' theory that we need to go through a process of "unfreezing" conceptions, then "freezing" them into a higher level of understanding (then repeat).

- Advocacy. Trial lawyers have been convincing a lot of people to change their minds towards certain facts and concepts for a long time. We might want to use advocacy techniques of letting our "jurors" figure things out for themselves (as opposed to whacking them over the head with our information), making our own best arguments (instead of continually arguing against other points of views), and even of using crisp language and short, focused communications in our work with busy adults.

- Psychology/Sociology. Many very smart people have long studied what motivates human beings and leads them to behave the way they do. One psychologist we in faith communities might pay particular attention to is Lev Vygotsky, who theorized that (my paraphrase) "you are who you hang out with." We are formed by those around us. And isn't that what the Body of Christ is about?

- Experiential Learning, including the School of Hard Knocks. How did you develop compassion? Chances are, it was something you experienced, at some point in your life. Might we then reflect on these experiences, connecting them to scripture and our values of faith (as suggested by Thomas Groome in his book,

*Christian Religious Education*)? Or do we need to help set up the experiences themselves (think "mission trips")?

If the Church is to survive, we might be wise to invest some time, some thought, and some bucks into workable means of transforming adults towards the full stature of Christ.

Christian Nurture in the Twenty-First Century

## Christian Formation of Adults —What's it All About?

In the Episcopal Church, we often think of adult Christian formation as the old "adult forum" offered by many parishes - a sage on a stage will lecture for forty minutes or so, perhaps followed by a handful of questions and a fairly brief discussion with parishioners. Maybe a parish will offer small group Bible studies or some other small group book group or support group.

Is that all we as a church have to offer? In a previous version of this webpage, I suggested that parishes offer a wider variety of large and small group adult formation programs, including book groups, film discussion groups, and perhaps even retreats and other "one shot" intensive programs.

Times they are a' changing. I would still love to see these kinds of programs, but in our current environment, I honestly don't see these kinds of programs happening, except for the largest and best staffed and funded parishes. So where does that leave us?

When one door closes, many windows often open. As the old adult forum method of Christian formation proves less and less effective for true lifelong Christian formation, I think we need to acknowledge other avenues of formation that indeed are already effective in helping many of us along on our journeys of faith. In acknowledging that faith formation happens largely out in the world, outside the walls of our parishes, we might better engage our own parishioners and newcomers in the journey of lifelong formation.

How do we learn? How are we continually formed, re-formed and transformed in faith and works? If you think about how you change your mind, change your actions, and see life with new perspective, you might find that your "formation" takes place in one of these ways:

**One-on-one communications and experiences**: Many of us change our minds and how we see the world as a result of knowing someone, hearing a story, seeing someone's struggles, making an observation, or seeing the actions of someone we might hope to emulate. We might remind ourselves to pay close attention to people and situations we find in our paths.

**The Media**: Many of us have long found ourselves influenced and challenged by books we read, movies we've seen, newspaper articles we've read. In this age of mass, instant communications, we as a church might acknowledge, embrace, and even produce stories that form us as human beings.

## Christian Nurture in the Twenty-First Century

**Spiritual Disciplines, including Worship:** Alongside any new media, we might deepen and enrich any transformative messages with ancient spiritual practices of liturgy, silence, devotional readings, and prayer. As Christians, these practices are still at the core of who we are and how we are transformed.

**Retreats, Pilgrimages, and other Intensive Formative Experiences:** As parishes are seemingly less and less able to provide "in-house" formation courses, this task might be (and already is, in many cases) more effectively and efficiently be taken up by diocesan, regional, and even national events, conferences, retreats, and pilgrimages. This strategy would allow planners to make well designed plans, offer excellent speakers and leaders, and would give participants the time and space to actively and intentionally work on spiritual formation.

**Intentional Study, Individually or in Small Groups:** As a curriculum designer myself, I won't throw the baby out with the bathwater. Many parishes are still offering excellent Bible studies. Many excellent curricula and resources are still being written and published. It would be crazy not to continue offering weekday or Sunday morning classes and study groups. What might be different is taking a hard look at when and where these programs are offered – schedules we've used for decades may not work anymore. People really do seem much,

much busier than in years before. Individual study programs are now published, and when all else fails for the busy road warrior, parent of small children, or other overwhelmed and time-limited person, individual studies or DVDs for home viewing could be a good thing.

With that said, new resources for adult Christian formation are published all the time. A primary role for a formation specialist would be to keep abreast of new offerings, vet them, and provide solid information on these resources to clergy and parish leaders.

Christian Nurture in the Twenty-First Century

## Lifelong Nourishing, Lifelong Transformations

I shared the parable of the Mustard Seed with my nursing home-bound father, who suffers a fairly advanced case of dementia. Although he was a bit agitated at first, he was clearly delighted with the colorful and eye-catching Godly Play materials I had brought with me. Even in his diminished mental state, we had a wonderful discussion. I had a chance to tell my father how little things he had said and done for his family and others would have a lasting effect on all of us, nurturing our lives and the lives of others we touched – perhaps all over the world – just like the speck of a mustard seed, growing as large as a two story house.

Later that afternoon, I presented the exact same parable materials to a small child who had been abandoned to an Eastern European orphanage at age 2 weeks. Just as my father had been able to discuss and deal with some end-of-life issues, this small boy was able to discuss and work on his own beginning-of-life issues. In his work, the ordinary man who sowed the seed is no longer in the picture, yet the seeds flourish nonetheless, nourished by the water and soil in which they are placed. The seeds grow by water and good soil and by grace and will give homes to other creatures. In this early childhood vision of the Kingdom of Heaven, all the little birds get homes.

The process of transformation is indeed lifelong. We are all working on our "stuff," and we will be working on all our various issues as long as we are alive. Work we do to intentionally engage ourselves and others in the stories of our lives and in hopes of ever moving forward is important in our early years, near our deaths, and at every stage of life in between.

To those working hard to prepare new opportunities for others to engage in these stories and do this intentional work, know that what you do is important – even the little things, even the details. Like mustard seeds, some things might be lost in the shuffle or fail to germinate, but others might produce thriving ministries you might not even know about or realize until years later.

At my father's nursing home, 70 and 80 year olds with Alzheimer's disease and dementia may not be able to talk, but almost all of them can still sing by heart hymns they learned in another century, at a time when my father farmed with a horse and plow. Seeds were planted in these souls that still nourish them, still give them comfort, even as they approach death and as their bodies barely function. Somebody taught them these songs – seemingly a little thing at the time. Somebody planted these seeds.

Christian Nurture in the Twenty-First Century

Cynthia Coe

**The Church in the Twenty-First Century:
Essays on Re-Thinking How We "Do" Church**

Cynthia Coe

Christian Nurture in the Twenty-First Century

**Garden Variety Christian Formation**

Two Stabs at a Model of Formation
– Good Try, But They Miss the Mark

Two very different models of formation have appeared on my laptop or tablet lately. Both had good points to make, but neither seemed to me a complete model of what formation in the 21$^{st}$ century needs to look like. Derek Olsen, in an Episcopal Café article, suggests that the resources needed are already available from a plethora of sources and simply need to be vetted, perhaps by a volunteer. Diana Butler Bass, in her excellent book *Christianity After Religion*, proposes mentoring relationships, whereby formation would take place one-on-one.

I am all in favor of online resources – I write them frequently. But these resources are simply tools of formation. Someone has to come up with the content, and content might be terrific; it might not be. Simply vetting the content will not make what we need for formation magically appear on the screen. One-on-one tutoring and mentoring is extremely useful, but collaborative learning and working and listening within groups is, I think, as much or perhaps more valuable. Thus, neither of these proposals provides direction for the ministry of formation or address current challenges and opportunities in this important work.

*Formation as Gardening*

As I was watering my little springtime garden and pondering what I could constructively say about this topic, I found a model for formation right smack in front of me – a garden. Jesus taught using gardening images: the mustard seed, the true vine, workers in the vineyard…the list goes on and on. Even the wine and bread of our Eucharist are agricultural products of wheat, water, and grapes.

Mature Christians don't just happen; somebody has to nurture them, tend to them, help keep them watered, and then even help figure out what to do with the fruits of the harvest. Spiritual formation is akin to cultivation of our gardens – planting seeds, waiting patiently for sprouts to appear, keeping young plants well watered and fertilized, then watching in awe as the harvest feeds others.

Formation is cultivation of the human soul. Formation is growth. Formation is cultivation of our congregations towards the full stature of Christ to provide abundant life for all.

So…how does our garden grow?

*Planning Needed*

We need a plan. Leaving folks to simply read whatever they find on the web seems to me much like walking into the forest to get your food and taking your chances – you might get fed, you might not. I sense that this is what happens in many of our parishes – adult (and even children and youth) formation can be a haphazard affair, based on the current interests of those in charge and the availability of speakers to come give a talk.

This may seem radical, but perhaps we need to take a look at what we want to "grow." What does a "mature Christian" look like? What do we consider nourishing "food" for all Christians? And don't we think we need to provide this "food" on an ongoing basis to maintain health and help our flocks grown towards the full stature of Christ?

In planning a garden, we might first decide what we want to serve, what we could reasonably grow in our soil, and how much time and space we have to devote to the task. Then, we would plant seeds (ordering them online, buying them at the local garden center, or even using heirloom seeds saved from the past). We would put these seeds in good soil, keep them watered, make sure the young plants had plenty of space to grow, and protect them from the weeds, pests, and wild animals. (There is, of course, no guarantee that our plan will "take." A lot is left up to the Holy Spirit and can be a mysterious process. Yet we will grow nothing if we do not plant seeds to begin with and undergo proper watering and maintenance.)

What we don't want is a diet of twinkies and junky canned foods. If we are going to provide Christian formation opportunities, we need to provide the good stuff. We need to give people what will help them grow, not a bunch of junk. What we think is luring children and adults with "fun!" and "entertainment" may actually be akin to feeding people with fatty, high sugar crap that will not help them grow in the Christian faith.

*Many Gardens, Many Gardeners*

Who will do the work to grow this spiritual food? That question could be answered in a multitude of ways and could vary in every little piece of God's kingdom. Much like Episcopal congregations, gardens and farms come in every size – vegetables planted in pots or planters, small backyard gardens, larger community gardens, and even large plots that feed thousands. All of these pieces of the earth can produce food – just in different ways. So it is with the ministry of formation: growth can take place almost anyplace, as long as seeds are planted in good soil and there is plenty of light and sunshine. (Growth generally will NOT take place if seeds stay in the dark, never get watered and are left in the basement, out of sight – as some formation programs are.)

Workers in the vineyard (or gardens) might be professionals, volunteers, or those who just have the passion for the work – as long as they are mindful of their jobs and get the work done. Do they have to be

Master Gardeners? No, but some good videos, books, and the availability of Master Gardeners to give advice would not be a bad thing. Like all gardening work, it's the time and attention that matters. (And time and attention to the ministry of formation may be sorely lacking in many congregations.)

Each garden, no matter its size, will have to be tended on the local level. When push comes to shove, someone needs to get down in the dirt and work. These tasks cannot be done remotely. Yes, we can buy our spiritual food in the market places, but that gets expensive (and we may not get the nutrition we really need). Could we hire gardeners? Sure. There is absolutely no reason why we couldn't hire professional teachers to do the skilled, dedicated work required to help people grow – schools do it all the time.

*Seed Companies and Garden Centers*

If we start a garden, we do need some supplies. Even if you have great soil and an abundant water supply for your garden, you'll likely need good seeds, a trowel, and a water hose or bucket to help you do your job. Formation, likewise, can best be done with quality seeds and tools. There are good resources and not-so-good resources for formation, just as there are fruitful seed varieties and others that might not germinate or might not be quite what we need. And as much as "programs" are dissed by the "faith is caught" school of thinking, the reality is that formation needs tried and true tools such as teaching methodologies to get the job done. (Just leaving the task to your own devices might be like trying to garden without a trowel or a defined garden space; you could do it, but it might not be effective or efficient.)

Just as heirloom seeds are growing in popularity, reclamation of traditions of the past might be seeds we would want to plant in our gardens. New technology makes new hybrids possible. We might want to consider grafting successful programs of the past onto new platforms of technology. Yet all these efforts take skill and time. Attempting these efforts would be akin to setting up a greenhouse or a trial garden – someone will need to provide the space and resources and give the gardeners a living wage to be able to sufficiently devote their time and skills to the task. Support of agriculture is often done by major state universities; the church might consider support of its own greenhouses to make sure proper development is done. (And leaving development up to for-profit corporations might not give us what we need. Making money and formation of Christians are usually not completely compatible.)

# Christian Nurture in the Twenty-First Century

*Workers in the Vineyard*

In the parable of the workers in the vineyard, the workers who came along late in the day got the same pay as those who had been around a long time. Why? Perhaps these workers were able to arrive on the scene with fresh eyes and new insight. They could look at the efforts of the longtime workers and see what worked and what could work better. Fresh eyes and energy are priceless.

As we endeavor to tend our gardens, I would hope we would look at the scene with fresh eyes. We might have ideas for new crops, new techniques, and new-fangled tools that just might lead to renewed growth, to a renewed church.

Christian Nurture in the Twenty-First Century

## "Spiritual Not Religious"
## – And If the Church Were Christian

Right before sitting down to write a review of *If the Church Were Christian* by Phillip Gulley, I picked up a copy of USA Today with the headline, "Young Adults Less Devoted to Faith." Are the two connected? As we in the church read and reflect on the grim factoids – 72% of young adults are "really more spiritual than religious;" 65% of young adults are either mushy Christians or Christians in name only – we need only face the deeper truths in *If the Church Were Christian* to have our collective "duh" moment.

Gulley holds up a mirror to Christians, asking whether we are doing what we say we are about. Much of his book is aimed at the more fundamentalist crowd, urging them to pay less attention to rules and judgment and more attention to mercy, kindness, and love of other human beings.

Other chapters could well apply to all churches. Gulley, a veteran Quaker pastor who has faced expulsion from his denomination for his criticism, takes the leadership of "the church" to task for being too comfortable in their own positions, failing to change with the times, and generally perpetuating a religious culture geared towards the entrenched and the insiders. As someone who obviously has pushed the buttons of his own denomination, he speaks passionately of the difficulties of changing the status quo of churches and of the ostricization of those who try.

For Episcopalians, we can give ourselves a modest pat on the back in response to much of Gulley's criticisms. We are fairly tolerant, we don't preach hell fire and damnation, and we're not really into the judgmental thing. Rules? We're more into the "use your brain and figure it out yourself" approach.

But then there's the innovation thing. We are, perhaps, not so good with the "change, grow, or die" approach. As we look at the sad statistics of adults ages 18-29 just not being served by the Church – even as they claim to be very "spiritual" – we might wonder if we are drifting more towards the "die" approach rather than the "change" or "grow" approaches.

Our numbers are down. Go to most Episcopalian events, and you will see mostly folks over the age of 50. There were exactly 4 kids in the Sunday School class my 6 year old attended this past Sunday, and that is in a community with a grossly overcrowded elementary school. Clearly, we are not reaching the spiritual yet not religious young adults chronicled in *USA Today* this morning.

But what if the Church put some resources into

## Christian Nurture in the Twenty-First Century

young adult ministry? What if the Church made these resources available for free to any parish that would use them? What if the Church made it a priority to reach out and welcome young adults into the congregation and then followed up with focused ministry geared specifically to them?

What if we had terrific Christian formation classes for children that engaged them and helped them learn the fundamentals of the Christian life and story? What if we had engaging parenting resources our parishioners say they want? What if we helped young adults address real life problems?

What if we became both a source and resource for well-grounded, authentic and meaningful spirituality to a generation that earnestly seeks spirituality? What if the church reclaimed its history of spirituality and reached out to the secular world with its storehouse of spiritual traditions and tools? What if these resources were re-tooled for the 21$^{st}$ century?

My husband works for a company in economically ravished Elkhart, Indiana. His company nonetheless turned a profit last year. Why? New product development – backed by full corporate support and resources. If the church likewise wants to survive in tough, tough times, new product development might be the way for it to go, too.

But first, the church needs to face the realities plainly printed on the front page of this morning's paper. Denial of problems usually does no one any good. Gulley might be faulted for being "too critical." But those who criticize care. Those who criticize passionately want to be agents of change for the better. This book is worth reading, if you care, too.

## Numbers – Do They Matter?

## Two Arguments, Pro and Con

You plan a class, a conference, a meeting – only a handful of people show up. Does that matter? I have very mixed feelings about this question. Obviously, you show hospitality, be present, and give it your all to those who do show up. But do you re-think your plans afterwards? I make the case for both positions. You decide.

*No, Numbers Don't Matter – Personal Ministry is Everything*

Jesus often taught one-on-one or in very small groups. The conversations with the woman at the well, Nicodemus, Zaccheus, and the numerous discussions Jesus had with his disciples were among his best and most enduring teachings.

Small numbers of people attending classes and conferences are a true blessing. You can have authentic conversations about subjects your attendees really want to talk about. Everyone gets plenty of your time and attention. If the conversation veers off topic and into a worthwhile subject you had not planned to cover, all the better.

Christian formation is often at its best when

done one-on-one or in very small groups. Micro Christian formation is also historically and Biblically rooted – Phillip teaching the Ethiopian man on the side of the road, the early Catechists mentoring new Christians, parents teaching their own children both in early Christian and in Jewish traditions.

Small numbers are like mustard seeds. Well tended and watered, the seeds you plant with even one person may grow and grow in that person to make a huge difference in the world. Even a short conversation may start a brand new ministry. You never know. Every conversation and teachable moment matters. The very best way to teach someone is one-on-one. Personal ministry is something we need to do more of.

*Yes, Numbers Matter a Lot – We Are Obligated to Make Good Stewardship of Resources*

As a DCE in a large church several years ago, I fretted over a couple of programs which attracted very few children and seemingly little interest or energy. I went to my rector for advice, and he asked, "do you know which denomination opens the largest number of new churches each year?" I correctly guessed the Southern Baptists. "And do you know which denomination closes the largest number of churches each year?" The Southern Baptists as well.

My rector's point was well taken – if you want to start a new ministry, you likely need to shut down another ministry that does not fulfill its mission. We all only have so many minutes in the day, and as God's call to us and as good stewards of resources and gifts given us, we need to make the most of our own time.

Under the First Amendment of the US Constitution, Americans have the right to attend any church they wish, or not. We cannot force them to attend our church programs; people are free to "vote with their feet" in all matters of church program attendance.

If people do not attend a Christian formation series, a conference, or a training course, perhaps there is a very good reason. It may not be a reason we care to face. We may not be doing our jobs in offering programs that meet interests or needs, we may not offer our best speakers or trainers, our programs may not be effective, or we might done our best job of publicizing the event in a very crowded media market. We may have simply botched the time or location of our event.

None of these factors are pleasant to face. None of us like to confess that perhaps we did not do a good job, much less that what we had to offer was not considered meaningful enough for people to spend their time on.

But humility is part of the Christian life and journey. Growth and change are, too. As part of God's call to each of us, we need to honestly confront what is needed by those we seek to serve, how best to do that, and who should take the lead. Those may not be answers we want to hear, much less act upon.

Jesus was not about protecting the status quo. Jesus was about radical change and doing things differently. If we truly want to spread Good News, we might have to follow Him in these respects as well.

Christian Nurture in the Twenty-First Century

## Mustard Seeds of Faith – Why Small Churches Might Not be as "Disadvantaged" as They Think

In talking to colleagues about the so-called "disadvantage" small churches might feel they have in ministering to others, I'm beginning to think small churches might actually have an advantage over the large churches. In small churches, people know each other. They have a sense of community. Things might not be as complicated – if you want to start a new program or ministry, you might not have to negotiate with 5 other ministries meeting at the same time in your church.

At a youth ministry conference I attended, the talk was all about "relational" ministry, not "programs." There was little talk of installing expensive, hot new curricula. Recommended pilgrimages included domestic road trips, rather than European odysseys. Small churches, the keynoter told us, are already "living the reality" of operating on less.

Fortunately, in this time of economic crisis, the internet levels the playing field for small churches drastically. Many quality free or low cost resources are now available by download. You can now get free lessons for all ages, a great teacher training text, and numerous other resources at the click of a mouse. Books on a multitude of topics are available for shipping anywhere in the country at relatively low cost via online bookstores,

205

and usually with free shipping.

All you need is a computer, and surely someone in every parish has a computer and would be willing to hit the print button. In fact, older parishioners might form friendships and mentoring relationships with younger people by simply asking for help in accessing these resources. (Teenagers LOVE to show up their parents and other adults with their vastly superior computer skills.)

And if you don't have a computer, put the word out that you could use a giveaway. Need Wifi? McDonald's, Starbucks, Kroger, Panera, and numerous other restaurants are glad for you to sit a spell and use theirs.

In this day and age, money is not necessarily a barrier to having a quality Christian formation ministry. And maybe it never was. As a DCE in a large, wealthy church, a generous parishioner donated ten thousand dollars to my program. I honestly couldn't figure out what to do with it; my programs were already well funded. What I needed was teachers willing to spend time preparing and ministering to children. What I needed was human beings willing to grow in faith and assist others so to do.

## Give Peace

## (And Denominational Resources) A Chance

Freedom is a good thing. Freedom is a quintessentially American value. We like to do what we want to do. We generally don't like someone else telling us what we should or should not do.

However, exercising our freedom to do as we like can often lead us out of community and even completely out of touch with those with whom we profess unity. We may think of ourselves as part of the family, but if we are not continually visiting our common values, we might – even unconsciously – find ourselves completely out of step with those with whom we hope to have unity.

Perusing a Christian Education Survey published not long ago, I did not see much unity, much community, or many shared values among our flock. A vast array of curricula and programs are used in our parishes, as seemingly each DCE or volunteer committee follows their own preferences. Thus, we have very little opportunity for resource sharing and not much more than a scintilla of common ground as to what we actually "do" in the way of teaching.

What difference does a curriculum" make, anyway? Who cares what kids are taught, as long as they are having fun and the volunteers are happy?

A curriculum is a "course to be run." A curriculum is a blueprint for what we feel is important as a community, a shared value system, a "to do" list of what we feel children of God of all ages should be taught. As a curriculum designer and writer myself, I can tell you that my values and theology absolutely DO go into my work. When I begin a project, I actually think, "how can I link this to the Baptismal Covenant and Holy Eucharist?" "How can I have people actually experience and think about certain scriptural concepts and Christian values?"

In the Episcopal Church, we use many, many curricula which are not designed by those steeped in our values and theology. And why is that a problem? Many of the curricula used by parishes are simply not in line with what we as Episcopalians believe, even in very generally terms. Many of these programs do not have any connection, introduction, or even use of the 1979 Book of Common Prayer, which is indeed the "blueprint" of our faith and does indeed represent our theology. Many conservative and even fundamentalist curricula present theologies contrary to our values, if you look beyond the fancy packages and claims of "fun" and "excitement."

If we want our children, youth, and adults to share our basic values - leaving plenty of room for diverse opinion as to how these values might be applied – we need to at the very least present, teach, and discuss these common values in the precious little times we have to spend with our flock. Why don't we?

Here's what I think is happening: parish Christian education folks might indeed try a resource provided by an Episcopal publisher or designer. The program musters low attendance, lackluster teaching, and generally "doesn't work." Volunteers show up unprepared. Attendance is sporadic.

So…the parish tries "something else." That "something else" might work a little better – for a while. Volunteers might find the program a bit more user friendly; it might seemingly have some bells and whistles that churn up a little more excitement – for a while. But generally speaking, the change in program does not solve the problem.

What *would* solve the problem? I respectfully suggest that the programs aren't the problems. I submit that the problems are these:

- Failure to uphold Christian formation as a priority

- Reliance on volunteer, unpaid teachers who do not have time to adequately study and prepare for lessons
- Low expectations
- Failure by clergy and bishops to insist or even require formational programs to be in line with our theology and to teach what we preach.

Not surprisingly, the most utilized program in our church, according to the 2010 survey, *Godly Play* (used by 21% of respondents, along with another 5% using the similar *Catechesis of the Good Shepherd*, a Roman Catholic designed program), requires training by teachers, provides professional training and support to those teaching in the field, and expects those using the program to maintain certain standards.

Apparently, something is going "right" with these programs, as substantially higher maintenance as they may be. Both *Godly Play* and *Catechesis* also teach liturgy, include periods of silent meditative time, and challenge children to really, really think and ponder scripture. They are not "fun" in the secular sense of the word, yet participants undoubtedly gain much in the way of spiritual and religious formation. (An outreach component of these programs would be appreciated, however.)

We need to give our own denomination a chance. We are generally pretty smart people. We have hard working Christian formation specialists who are up to the task of designing great programs and curricula. But...they could use some help and support.

## Growing Seeds of Hope

Not long ago I read a story of refugees, originally from southern Sudan, who had just returned to their homeland after years of living in exile abroad. They were faced with the immediate challenge of building communities from scratch and figuring out how to feed themselves. Yet few of these refugees knew how to farm; only the elderly remembered the basics of vital life skills.

As the 21$^{st}$ century progresses, the Church might find itself in a similar position. In an era of post-Christendom, younger generations who practice the faith will likely not have the "basics" of the faith under their belts. Like the newly arrived refugees in southern Sudan, these younger generations will most certainly come up with many new innovations, and Christianity might not look much like the Christianity we knew in the 20$^{th}$ century. As the Church struggles to find itself again, mistakes will likely be made as well, and subsequent generations might find that it sure would be nice to have the resource of experience and wisdom around to help them along.

We might ask ourselves what "seeds" we are producing to help subsequent generations along. How are we nurturing those younger than ourselves? What teachable moments do we seize? How are we being intentional in passing along our wisdom and knowledge to others? Are we effectively using new technologies and effective methods? What are we teaching our children about the practice of our Baptismal Covenant?

In our ministries of Christian formation, are we truly passing along the faith to others? Do we have quality programs and tools in place, or are we merely "keeping the kids quiet and out of the way while we have our peaceful worship service"? Are we passing along the importance of truly ministering to others in need? When younger people among us have moments of crisis, to what and to whom will they turn?

A friend of mine who worked at TVA here in Knoxville told me that the management philosophy of this agency was that "you should always be training those working for you to do your job." This process of training and enabling others to take your place might push buttons with many of us. To do this, we have to acknowledge that we will not be around forever. We may find ourselves moving on to different tasks or locations. We may find ourselves engaging in lives we never would have expected for ourselves. We may even find ourselves obsolete.

Letting go of our presumed indispensability could, however, turn out to be a liberating experience, too. As we pass our torches, we could – if we have done our jobs of training others to take our places – look with great satisfaction at younger people living into their own gifts and contributing talent and energy we never dreamed possible. Just like a farmer, we could look at the seeds we have planted and see new growth and a bountiful harvest all around us.

But before these seeds are planted, the plant must mature, let the seeds drop onto new earth, then wait patiently and in hope for new growth to appear.

Christian Nurture in the Twenty-First Century

## ACKNOWLEDGMENTS

I am incredibly appreciative of my husband, Tom, for his unwavering support of my work. I also appreciate so much the bright and shining lights of faith shared by my parents, H. Rhea and Mary Lawson, throughout their lives. I tremendously appreciate the opportunity to parent my three children and to see what Christian Nurture looks like in real life.

This book was first written as my Master of Arts thesis while at Virginia Theological Seminary. I am very appreciative to Amy Geary Dyer, George Kroupa, and Dorothy Linthicum for their guidance and for sharing their wisdom during these years.

The Essays in Christian Formation were written as blog posts for my website, ETChristianFormation.org, over the last several years. I am grateful for all those who took time to read, comment, and discuss these ideas.

Finally, I am tremendously appreciative to all the children, young people, and adult teachers and volunteers who worked with me over the past several years. I learned so much through your work, your stories, and your ministries shared with me and with each other.

## ABOUT THE AUTHOR

Cynthia Coe is a writer and curriculum developer based in Knoxville, Tennessee. An honors graduate of Virginia Theological Seminary, she also holds a law degree with honors and an undergraduate degree with highest honors from the University of Tennessee.

After serving as a parish Director of Children's Ministries at the Episcopal Church of the Ascension in Knoxville, Cynthia Coe served as Formation Consultant to Episcopal Relief & Development, writing and developing the Abundant Life Garden Project® curriculum resources, along with curriculum resources on malaria prevention awareness and resources to help children and their adult leaders cope with disaster situations.

In 2014-2016, she serves as an Environmental Stewardship Fellow of the Episcopal Church, writing and developing curriculum resources to lead children and youth in creation care. She is the mother of three children.

## Notes

[1] William P. Haugaard, "The Continental Reformation of the Sixteenth Century," ed. John H. Westerhoff III and O.C. Edwards, Jr., *A Faithful Church: Issues in the History of Catechesis* (Wilton, CT: Morehouse-Barlow Co., Inc., 1981), p. 137.
[2] Ibid., p. 145 (quoting Elector John at the 1530 Diet of Augsburg).
[3] Luke 18:17, *The New Oxford Annotated Bible, New Revised Standard Version* (New York: Oxford, 1991).
[4] Matthew 19:14 (NRSV); *see also* Mark 10:13-16; Luke 18:15-17.
[5] *See, e.g.,* James Fowler, *Stages of Faith* (San Francisco:HarperCollins, 1995), p. 122-134.
[6] Matthew 18:3 (NRSV).
[7] Sophia Cavalletti, *The Religious Potential of the Child* (Chicago: Catechesis of the Good Shepherd Publications, 1992), p. 30-46.
[8] Matthew 18:6-7 (NRSV).
[9] *See* Daniel B. Stevick, *Baptismal Moments; Baptismal Meanings* (New York: The Church Hymnal Corporation, 1987), p. 8; *see also* John L. Elias, *A History of Christian Education: Protestant, Catholic, and Orthodox Perspectives* (Malabar, FL: Krieger Publishing Company, 2002), p. 1.
[10] Stevick, p. 7.
[11] Ibid.
[12] Stevick, p. 8; *see also* Maxwell E. Johnson, *The Rites of Christian Initiation* (Collegeville, MN: The Liturgical Press, 1999), p. 36-27.
[13] Stevick, p. 8.
[14] Galatians 6:6 (NRSV).
[15] *The New Oxford Annotated Bible, New Revised Standard Version* (New York: Oxford, 1991), p. 270 NT, note 6.6.
[16] *The Didache*, translated and annotated by James A. Kleist (New York: Paulist Press, 1948), Section 13, p. 23.
[17] Ibid.
[18] *See also* Ephesians 4:11 and Romans 12:7.
[19] James 3:1 (NRSV).
[20] *The Didache*, note 93, page 164-165.
[21] Ibid., p. 164.

[22] Ibid., p. 165.
[23] Ibid., Introduction, p. 3.
[24] Ibid., Sections 11-13, p. 22-23.
[25] Ibid., Section 4:9, p. 17.
[26] Deuteronomy 6:7 (NRSV).
[27] Vigen Guroian, "The Ecclesial Family: John Chrysostom on Parenthood and Family," ed. Marcia J. Bunge, *The Child in Christian Thought* (Grand Rapids: William B. Eerdmans Publishing Company, 2001), p. 69.
[28] Ibid.,68, 66; *see also* Kendig Brubaker Cully, ed., *Basic Writings in Christian Education* (Philadelphia: The Westminster Press, 1960), p. 52-57.
[29] Ibid., 64, 75.
[30] *See* James E. Reed and Ronnie Prevost, *A History of Christian Education* (Nashville: Broadman and Holman Publishers, 1993), p. 70.
[31] Stevick, p. 10.
[32] Leonel L. Mitchell, "The Development of Catechesis in the Third and Fourth Centuries: From Hippolytus to Augustine," ed. John H. Westerhoff III and O. C. Edwards, Jr., *A Faithful Church: Issues in the History of Catechesis* (Wilton, CT: Morehouse-Barlow Co, Inc., 1981), p. 49.
[33] Ibid., p. 52.
[34] Reed and Prevost, p. 81-87.
[35] Ibid., p. 91.
[36] Ibid., p. 98-99.
[37] Milton McC. Gatch, "Basic Christian Education from the Decline of Catechesis to the Rise of the Catechisms," *A Faithful Church*, p. 79-80.
[38] Ibid., p. 81.
[39] Ibid., p. 89.
[40] Ibid., p. 88.
[41] Ibid.
[42] Ibid., p. 87-88.
[43] Ibid., p. 103.
[44] William P. Haugaard, "The Continental Reformation of the Sixteenth Century," *A Faithful Church*, p. 109.
[45] Ibid., p. 113.
[46] Ibid., p. 119.

47 Ibid., p. 120.
48 Ibid., p. 122.
49 Ibid., p. 127.
50 Ibid., p. 123.
51 Ibid., p. 132-133.
52 Ibid., p. 137.
53 Reed and Prevost, p. 192-193. *See also* Jane E. Strohl, "The Child in Luther's Theology," *The Child in Christian Theology*, p. 150-152.
54 Strohl, p. 152.
55 Haugaard, p. 145.
56 Barbara Pitkin, "'The Heritage of the Lord':Children in the Theology of John Calvin," *The Child in Christian Thought*, p. 174.
57 Haugaard, p. 146.
58 Ibid., p. 145.
59 Ibid., p. 147.
60 Fredrica Harris Thompsett, "Godly Instruction in Reformation England: The Challenge of Religious Education in the Tudor Commonwealth," *A Faithful Church*, p. 191.
61 Thompsett, p. 197, quoting English reformer Thomas Becon.
62 Ibid., p. 198.
63 Ibid.
64 Ibid., p. 186-187.
65 Ibid., p. 180.
66 Reed and Prevost, p. 295.
67 Thompsett, p. 264.
68 Ibid.
69 Reed and Prevost, p. 257.
70 Ibid., p. 257-258.
71 Ibid., p. 275-276.
72 Richard P. Heitzenrater, "John Wesley and Children," *The Child in Christian Thought*, p. 290-291.
73 Reed and Prevost, p. 259-260.
74 John E. Booty, "Since the Reformation: An Emphasis on the American Experience," *A Faithful Church*, p. 272-273.
75 Booty, p. 273.

[76] *Christian Nurture* appeared in various forms between 1847 and 1861. Bushnell's last expansion of his ideas about children and their faith were published in a 1861 book edition.
[77] Horace Bushnell, *Christian Nurture* (New Haven: Yale University Press, 1888; 1947 edition).
[78] Robert Prichard, *A History of the Episcopal Church* (Harrisburg, PA: Morehouse Publishing, 1999), p. 180.
[79] Ibid., p. 216.
[80] Ibid., p. 231-232.
[81] John H. Westerhoff, III, *Will Our Children Have Faith?* (Harrisburg, PA: Morehouse Publishing, revised 2000 ed.), p. 6-9.
[82] Ibid., p.56. *See also* Kenda Creasy Dean and Ron Foster, *The Godbearing Life: The Art of Soul Tending for Youth Ministry* (Nashville: Upper Room Books, 1998).
[83] *Catechesis of the Good Shepherd* is a Montessori-based children's Christian education program developed by Roman Catholic laywoman Sophia Cavalletti. Children to work at their own pace with "hands-on" figures of Biblical figures and liturgical objects in a quiet, meditative retreat environment.
[84] *Godly Play* is also a Montessori-based program for children developed by Jerome Berryman, an Episcopalian priest. Berryman trained as a catechist and Montessorian in Italy, then developed his own program similar to *Catechesis of the Good Shepherd*. He has contributed to this method by added emphasis on open-ended wondering and art responses by children in response to stories presented to them.
[85] Gabriel Moran, *Showing How: The Act of Teaching* (Valley Forge, PA: Trinity Press International, 1997), p. 153.
[86] Loren B. Mead, *The Once and Future Church* (Washington, D.C.: The Alban Institute, 1991), p. 49-53.
[87] Robert D. Putnam, *Bowling Alone: The Collapse and Revival of American Community* (New York: Simon & Schuster, 2000), p. 72; *see also* Loren B. Mead, *Transforming Congregations for the Future* (Bethesda, MD: The Alban Institute, 1994), p. 1-12.
[88] Putnam, p. 78.

[89] Jack L. Seymour and Donald E. Miller, "Agenda for the Future," *Mapping Christian Education: Approaches to Congregational Learning* (Nashville: Abingdon Press, 1997), p. 113.
[90] Putnam, p. 189.
[91] Karen S. Peterson, "Parents Feel They're Failing to Teach Values," *USA Today*, October 30, 2002, Section D, p. 1.
[92] Ibid.
[93] Karen S. Peterson, "For Parents, Advice Overkill," *USA Today*, October 30, 2002, Section D, p. 6.
[94] David S. Schuller, ed., *Rethinking Christian Education: Explorations in Theory and Practice* (St. Louis, MO: Chalice Press, 1993), p. 33.
[95] Loren B. Mead, *The Once and Future Church* (Washington, D.C.: The Alban Institute, 1991), p. 8.
[96] Tom Beaudoin, *Virtual Faith: The Irreverent Spiritual Quest of Generation X* (San Francisco: Jossey-Bass, 1998), p. 51-52.
[97] Beaudoin, p. 41.
[98] Beaudoin, p. 117.
[99] Beaudoin, p. 168-169.
[100] Beaudoin, p. ix.
[101] For an excellent discussion of how social trends develop, *see* Malcolm Gladwell, *The Tipping Point: How Little Things Can Make a Big Difference* (New York: Little, Brown and Company, 2000).
[102] Deuteronomy 6: 5-6 (NRSV).
[103] Deuteronomy 6:7 (NRSV).
[104] Deuteronomy 6:7-9 (NRSV).
[105] Deuteronomy 11:19 (NRSV).
[106] *Book of Common Prayer* (New York: Oxford University Press, 1990), p. 302.
[107] Id.
[108] Matthew 18:5 (NRSV); *see also* Luke 9:48; Mark 9:37.
[109] Ibid., 304-305.
[110] I Corinthians 12:12-26 (NRSV)
[111] I Corinthians 12:29 (NRSV).
[112] James 3:1 (NRSV).
[113] Luke 21:37 (NRSV).

[114] Beaudoin, p33.
[115] Harris, Maria, *Fashion Me a People: Curriculum in the Church* (Louisville, KY: Westminster/John Knox Press, 1989).

[116] James Michael Lee, ed., *Forging a Better Religious Education in the Third Millennium* (Birmingham, AL: Religious Education Press, 2000).
[117] *See ,e.g.,* Burton L. White, *The New First Three Years of Life* (New York: Simon & Schuster, 1995).
[118] Gabriel Moran, *Showing How :The Act of Teaching* (Valley Forge, PA: Trinity Press International, 1997), p. 159.
[119] *See* Lucie W. Barber, *The Religious Education of Preschool Children* (Birmingham, AL: Religious Education Press, 1981), p. 13 ("Parents as Paraprofessionals").
[120] *See* Beaudoin, p. 33.
[121] *See* Norma Cook Everist, "Issues and Ironies of the New Millennium," *Forging A Better Religious Education in the New Millennium* (Birmingham, AL: Religious Education Press, 2000) p. 61.
[122] *See* Richard Kew and Roger White, *Toward 2015: A Church Odyssey* (Boston: Cowley Publications, 1997) p. 36.
[123] Stephanie Armour, "More Americans put families ahead of work," *USA Today*, December 5, 2002, Section A, p. 1.
[124] Karen S. Peterson, "Extracurricular burnout," *USA Today*, November 19, 2002, Section D, p. 7.
[125] Karen S. Peterson, "Parents Feel They're Failing to Teach Values," *USA Today*, October 30, 2002, Section D, p. 1.
[126] *See* Martin E. Marty, "Christian Education in a Pluralistic Culture," *Rethinking Christian Education*, ed. David S. Schuller (St. Louis, MO: Chalice Press, 1993), p. 19.
[127] Id.
[128] The magi appear in the Gospel of Matthew but not in the Gospel of Luke, though many Nativity stories collapse the two Gospels stories into one story and have all the characters appear at once.

[129] William P. Haugaard, "The Continental Reformation of the Sixteenth Century," *A Faithful Church*, p. 137.
[130] *Abington School District v. Schempp* and *Murray v. Curlett*, 374 U.S. 203 (1963).
[131] *See* Thomas H. Groome, *Education for Life: A Spiritual Vision for Every Teacher and Parent* (Allen, TX: Thomas More, 1998).
[132] *Book of Common Prayer*, p. 303.
[133] James Michael Lee, "CCD Renewal," ed. D. Campbell Wyckoff, *Renewing the Sunday School and the CCD* (Birmingham, AL: Religious Education Press, 1986), p. 240.
[134] Id., p. 239.
[135] Id., p. 240.
[136] Id., p. 238.
[137] Gabriel Moran, *Showing How: The Act of Teaching* (Valley Forge, PA: Trinity Press International, 1997), p. 211.
[138] Resolution 1985-A099, Substitute Canon III.26, General Convention, *Journal of the General Convention of The Episcopal Church, Anaheim, 1985* (New York: General Convention, 1986), p. 584. The concept of licensed catechists was re-affirmed by subsequent General Conventions in 1988 and 2000.
[139] Id.
[140] *Called to Teach and Learn*, p. 180-181.
[141] *See* Maria Harris and Gabriel Moran, *Reshaping Religious Education: Conversations on Contemporary Practice* (Louisville, KY: Westminster John Knox Press, 1998), p.49.

www.ingramcontent.com/pod-product-compliance
Lightning Source LLC
Chambersburg PA
CBHW022112040426
42450CB00006B/669